FOUL BERTHS AND FRENCH SPIES

Essays on the Port of Liverpool c1800-1930

Adrian Jarvis

NATIONAL MUSEUMS LIVERPOOL

2003

Published 2003
by
National Museums Liverpool,
Merseyside Maritime Museum,
Albert Dock, Liverpool L3 4AQ.

© National Museums Liverpool

British Library Cataloguing-in-Publication Data
A catalogue record of this book is available from the British Library

ISBN 1-902700-21-X

Typeset by Milepost Research,
41 Fountain Street, Accrington BB5 0QR.

CONTENTS

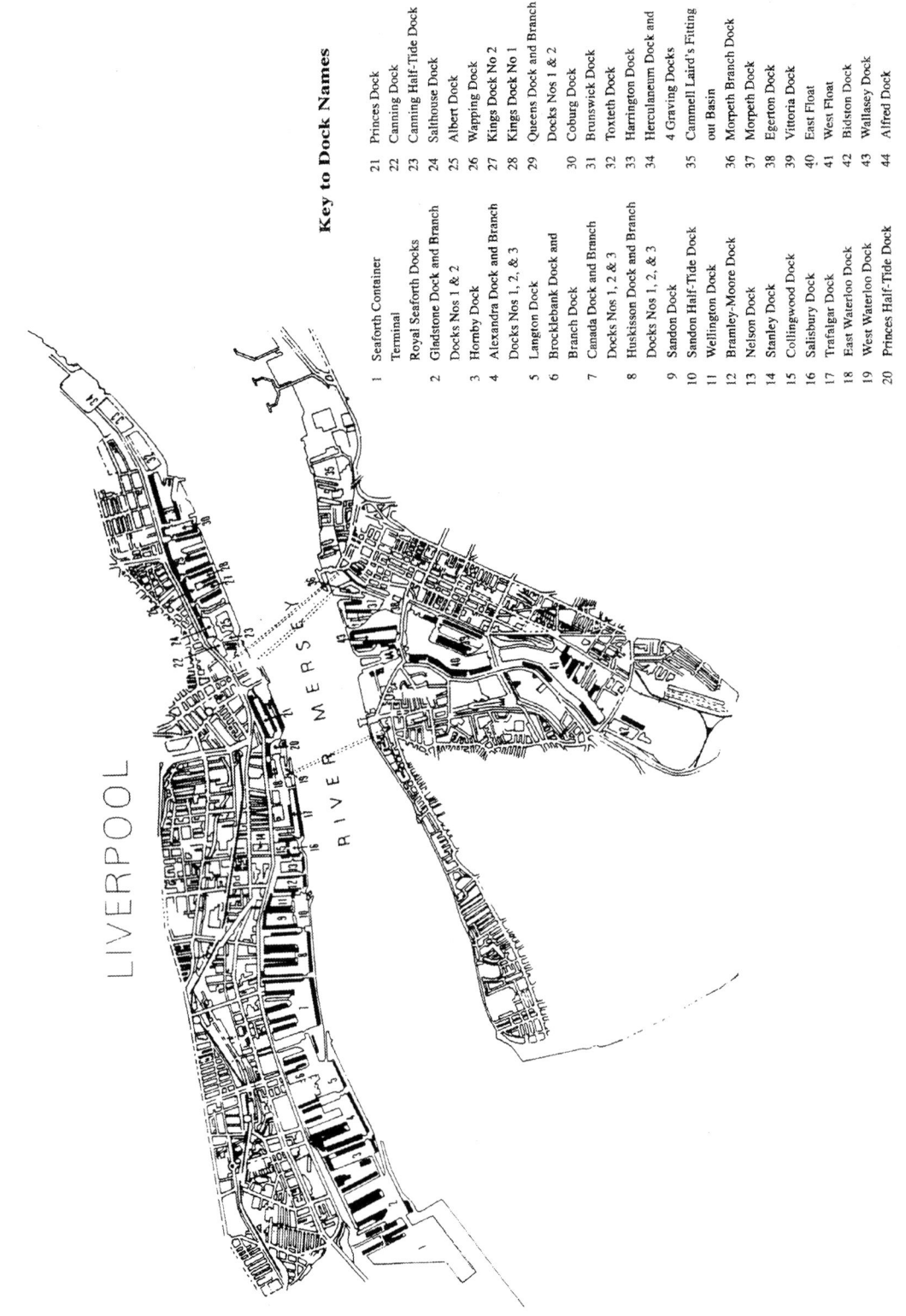

LIVERPOOL

RIVER MERSEY

Introduction

When one sets out to research a book, there are always pieces of extra information which are hoarded because they might be useful one day. This seems a wasteful process, but there are few more basic historical mistakes than having to spend days trying to re-trace some crucial reference or statistic whose location you failed to record the first time you found it. The danger of this approach is ending up with masses of useless and themeless information, which only provides a temptation to strike off at tangents.

That is why conferences are useful. They allow the author to pick out some theme which has been or is to be treated in his or her hardback book (whether published or in preparation) and pursue it further to produce a more detailed and tightly-focussed paper. All but one of the papers in this small collection were originally written for maritime history conferences in various parts of the world, though the attentive reader will undoubtedly detect bits which have appeared in a shorter form in either my *Liverpool Central Docks* or my *Liverpool Dock Engineers*. There will be small sneak previews of my forthcoming book on the Port of Liverpool 1905-38. At a conference one normally gets to discuss ideas with like-minded people (that is, after all, what conferences are for) and it is well-known that the informal discussions over breakfast or in the bar at night are sometimes more enlightening than the formal discussions of papers in the sessions. The fruits of many discussions of both kinds are incorporated here.

The danger in producing a collection of conference papers is that they can easily lack any sense of unity, or underlying theme, and the papers here presented may so appear at first sight. But they do have a common theme, which is that they all question established views to a greater or lesser degree. Of course not all of the text in every paper is questioning an established view, because on some subjects there is no such view unless it be held that I have just established it here.

Over the last two decades, large amounts of port archive material to which access was previously difficult (or even impossible) have been lodged in public depositories and thus become much more available to scholars. Hence after a certain time-lag, research into the history of ports has grown extremely rapidly, producing a concomitant increase in the published literature. As recently as 1990, conference papers and papers in learned journals on port history were quite thin on the ground, whereas now it is difficult to attend a maritime history conference or pick up a journal and not find something about ports in it. This is a situation in which I am not guiltless, but neither is the responsibility confined to people like myself who have sought to know more about one port, looking at others only fairly perfunctorily by way of comparison.

On the contrary, we have seen the appearance of the truly international port historian, of whom the archetype was the late Frank Broeze, a native of the Netherlands and an adopted Australian, who seemed equally at home researching the history of ports of the Indian Ocean, East Asia, the Persian Gulf: truly a Renaissance Man among port historians. Lewis Fischer of Newfoundland has moved into the field of comparative port history, again on a worldwide basis, and one thing which these two distinguished scholars have in common is their extraordinary productivity.

Gordon Jackson has published less, but no summary of the recent development of port history could omit his *History and Archaeology of Ports*, a book which undermined simultaneously the twin perils of geographical determinism and 'bosses' history'. The former might be aphorised as 'a port is like it is because of where it is', an argument brushed off by Jackson with his well-known *obiter dictum* 'in the final analysis, a port is not a place but a community of merchants'. Perhaps even more importantly, he did not automatically accept that ports were designed, constructed, operated and used by gentlemen, and intelligent ones at that. Put like that it sounds obvious, but a cluster of house histories of major ports cited in Paper 3, below, took pretty exactly that point of view and in so far as port history penetrated more general local or economic history at all, it carried that flavour with it. Common sense and experience tells us that there were good and bad, brilliant and stupid, men involved in these as in most human activities.

Investigating such questions requires getting down to a very fine level of detail in the archives, and that soon reveals that almost everything in port engineering and management was far more complex than we had previously realised. Even such 'well-known' stories as that of the application of hydraulic power to cargo-handling, dock gate driving and other purposes, which was made necessary by the increasing size of ships in the late nineteenth century, were not in fact well-enough known, and the first paper in this collection points out two reversals of the truth, one of them by a fairly exact 180°. In each case the mistake arose not from the author's idleness or stupidity but from his not having consulted the right documents.

Archivists love minute books: faced with a collection of paper which will not fit into their stores they will 'weed' practically anything in preference to minute books. Given a box of red stickers to identify things to be saved first in the event of fire or flood they will stick them on minute books. In a sense that is quite right, but minutes are often so brief and formulaic as to provide very little information about what was *really* happening. They are basically documents for outsiders, those outside that inner caucus which wields the real power. I

had not been long in the business of researching the history of the Port of Liverpool before I realised that a greater-than-usual brevity in the Minutes covering any particular subject was a reliable indicator that something was afoot which the outsiders were not meant to know about. Returning to hydraulics, the source which revealed that the application of hydraulic power to entrance gates was a matter of time, not of labour costs, was an Engineer's Commonplace Book, a document which, in the normal order of things, would never be seen even by the Chairman of the Works Committee, much less by outsiders.

An underlying theme throughout 'Steam Begat Steam' is that in the late nineteenth century it was necessary for ports to be in a continuum of extension and modernisation of their infrastructure: that the only way ports could stay in business in the period roughly 1850-1930 was by building facilities for ever larger and larger ships, and that it became necessary to plan these facilities with increasing excess capacities made necessary by the acceleration in the growth of ship sizes. To look, in short, further into the future. This was long an accepted view, and remains in general terms correct, but this collection is about questioning, and the second paper suggests that the case was not as simple as that: the throughput (in tons per yard of quay per year) of some of the improvements made to the Liverpool Docks between 1873 and 1905 rises much less than might be expected. New docks did not *necessarily* do better than old ones, nor docks designed for larger vessels better than those for smaller ones. If we measure revenue per yard of quay instead the results are less counter-intuitive but still fall rather short of completely substantiating the former 'invest or die' interpretation. The four projects here taken as case studies show benefit to the revenues of the port in almost inverse order of their cost and their cost/benefit to be fairly clearly so. Of course, when we look at matters in a detached manner, this is how it should be, because the further the Board and its engineers tried to look into the future, the more likely they were to get it wrong.

The third paper is a cautionary piece about relying too much on efficiency figures like those used in the second, which in turn depends again on our relying too much on face values. The paper recognises, for the first time, that we cannot even believe official statements of the size of the port. The effects of engineering work impinging on operation have long been recognised (though probably under-estimated) but there were many other factors which reduced the available capacity of the port. One of these was rubbish. At any given time in the period studied something of the order of $\frac{1}{2}$% of the entire land area of the dock estate was occupied by rubbish. Taken together, the various wastage of land and water space amounted to approximately one eighth of the working capacity of the docks. The entire elimination of this waste could never be achieved in practice, but if it were possible, the theoretical result would be the availability of more additional space than was provided when the entire Gladstone system opened its 54 acres of water for business!

The fourth paper came into being through another case of my suspicions being aroused by the absence of information in the archives. Having decided I ought to know a little about the early days of oil importing on the Mersey, I innocently sought figures for landings. Those for conventional cargoes were readily available in tabular form for part of the period and were recorded in the minutes of the Docks & Quays Committee for the rest. But not for bulk petroleum products in the 1920s. I eventually found that they *did* exist in the Committee Papers for the Docks & Quays Committee, but the minutes themselves not only did not transcribe them but did not even allude to their being presented to the meetings. This immediately suggests an intention to keep the press in the dark, because such an allusion would have been made during the 'Public Business' when the reporters were present: the contents of the support papers were known only to Members, a handful of the most trusted officers, and the Committee Clerks who wrote

them. What could be the dark secret of the new Dingle Oil Jetties?

It was, surprisingly, success. Normally, when one finds an attempted or an actual cover-up and succeeds in getting to the bottom of the matter, it is failure or dishonesty which is being concealed. Not here: Dingle was a roaring success and what the Board apparently did not want known was just how much of its total revenue was coming from two cheap wooden jetties and how relatively little from its hugely expensive docks. This prompts a return to my old theme of the maintenance of credit-worthiness being the key responsibility of the Board: how easy would it be to borrow new capital to complete Gladstone or embark on other major projects which were already envisaged if it were known that although the whole cost of the Dingle Jetty had been less than that of just one linear foot of the three-storey transit sheds at Gladstone, not counting the cost of the foot of quayside it stood on, it was already (in its first year's operation) handling 320 tons/yard and rising?

The reasoning was praiseworthy and the covering-up done in what I think the Members legitimately believed were the best interests of the port as a whole, because trade was bound to recover eventually, and then the spendid facilities at Gladstone would come into their own. In principle they were right, though trade recovery took longer than expected, and the higher efficiency of the new berths at Gladstone almost certainly helped in the Board's survival of the troubled times.[1]

The fifth paper is one which arose entirely by accident, and may, indeed, be thought a self-indulgence in the manner mentioned above. It was when researching a paper on the dock construction workers that I first took an interest in nineteenth century professional literature on the optimisation of muscle power. Much simplified, the conclusion of most such writing was that the traditional British navvy was expensive in wages but capable of moving proportionately large amounts of spoil, and hence good value. One of the comparisons encountered several times was that between such 'proper' navvies and convict labour. I allowed myself to stray into the subject a little and soon discovered that the use of convict labour was peculiar to dock and harbour schemes funded and managed by national government. The confusions in government policy towards both the works and the convicts contrast markedly with the single-mindedness of commercial port construction, here exemplified for the sake of brevity by comparison with the works of Jesse Hartley. Though many other examples could have been chosen, I could not resist the irony that one of Liverpool's sillier historical myths is that Hartley employed French prisoners of war - told in one case of a building completed in 1848!

A peripheral subject, perhaps, but Gordon Jackson and I have often remarked on the absence of a government policy towards the port services industry. This paper may be thought to provide a sidelight on that position, by showing how fortunate the industry was in being left to get along with only the shipping industry, and not government as well, to burden it with useless advice and constant interference.

The final paper is an exploration of one of the 'nooks and crannies' which began life during the preparation of a dayschool contribution on the subject of visitors' accounts of Liverpool. It is one of the clichés of local history to quote Defoe's opinion of the place in question, and the intention here is to provide and interrogate the text of two hitherto unused accounts of visits to Liverpool with regard to their purpose, accuracy and usefulness.

Does any of this matter?

If we accept that there is some purpose in knowing about and understanding history then it becomes difficult to deny that the history we know should be as correct as we can get it in both fact and interpretation. As mentioned above, it is not hard to find statements in print which are not merely slightly inaccurate but are the exact reverse of the truth. It used to be thought, for example,

that when Liverpool Corporation sold the land on which Birkenhead Docks were to be built, they had been duped into enabling a competitor on their doorstep.[2] Twenty five years passed before a contribution to a discussion of a paper at the Institution of Civil Engineers revealed that at the time of the sale the vendors knew there was quicksand under the site and the purchasers did not: could this be? Another 130 years passed before anybody (namely me) asked that question. The confirmation was a matter of the exact timing of the payments: upon what might be thought an irrelevant detail hung the question of whether the Liverpool Corporation was made up of fools (one local newspaper went so far as to liken them to babies) or of extremely ruthless and successful businessmen. The Birkenhead scheme ran into phenomenal over-spends and was effectively bankrupted — exactly as the 'babies' had intended, suggesting that the latter view is correct.

These things matter because they colour our view on other issues: if, for example, we thought that the Dock Committee members were stupid then we might assume that the eschewal of convict labour was stupid too. As is argued below, convict labour might be useful in some cases, but the construction of merchant dock systems, under intense time-pressure, was certainly not one of them.

There is a simpler and more fundamental reason for studying these minutiae. Every work of port history that I know of which was published before Jackson's *History and Archaeology of Ports* depends mainly or even exclusively for both narrative and interpretation on the use of source material which does not tell us how a port really worked, but only how people wished us to believe that it worked. Accounts of failures, overspends or even occasional downright corruption are few, complaints (often derived from newspaper correspondence columns) about pilferage by dock labourers are many. I am not a labour historian, but some of the quantities of goods (particularly of coffee beans) said to have been pilfered would have been physically impossible by the means suggested. The historian who has started out from the assumption that dock labourers are the only dishonest people working in the port is unlikely to consider the possibility that 'pilferage' was in fact the cover for comparatively large-scale white-collar smuggling. The irony is that it was only because dock labourers were widely regarded as congenital thieves and liars that this particular form of smuggling was possible: it depended on persuading the Customs man that goods should be written off as stolen when in fact they had been disguised and carted away under false paperwork.

Even when we find a dose of candour, as in the case of Mountfield's account of the 'rather serious under-estimate' in the re-construction of Alfred Entrances at Birkenhead, we find the exact nature of the problem (which was a major failing in internal communications) is hedged around, and we certainly do not learn that some of the blasting was so incompetently executed as to break every window within about 300 yards — a costly error since it included the appropriately-named 'glass house' at Wallasey Lairage.[3] This is good old-fashioned bosses' history: it is not actually false and it is not malicious, but through excision of the detail of what was really happening, it is misleading, some might say seriously so.

A Note on Sources

Prominent among the archival collections mentioned above as being comparatively recently placed in public depositories is the enormous Mersey Docks & Harbour Board collection in the Maritime Archives & Library, Merseyside Maritime Museum. Unless otherwise specified, all unpublished material cited in this book is in that collection.

Steam begat Steam: the effect of steam shipping on the technology of ports.[4]

The changes in typical dimensions of ocean-going ships which resulted from the adoption of first paddle steamers and later screw steamers are sufficiently well-known and documented to require only passing mention. The problems these changes created for dock engineers are also fairly straightforward and well-documented, and similarly need no lengthy explanation.[5]

The principal problem paddle steamers posed was that they got wider with remarkable rapidity. The largest of the Black Ball Line's transatlantic sailing packets (*Great Western*) had a beam of 40ft 6in. By the late 1850s a large Transatlantic paddler (such as the Collins Line's *Adriatic*), while having a beam of only around 50ft, was 75-80ft over the paddle boxes.[6] This meant that port authorities were faced with three choices: building new facilities for them, making enormous and costly alterations to old facilities or losing an extremely prestigious and potentially very profitable trade. There was a secondary problem, which was that steamers largely succeeded (with the exception of the really long voyages to Australia and the Far East) in creaming off the high-value trades, which meant that sail could often only compete by being cheap. This in turn meant that sailing ships generally got bigger, slower and deeper, causing problems analogous to those brought later and more acutely by the screw steamer.

If the paddle steamer was bad news for port authorities, the screw steamer was much worse, because it got bigger mostly by being deeper rather than longer or wider, producing a variant of the same dilemma as the paddle steamer but with the added twist that where expensive new works had been constructed wide and shallow for paddle steamers, they were of use only for relatively small screw steamers. Drafts rose steadily throughout the latter half of the century, to the point where long-haul cargo liners commonly drew as much as 30ft fully laden, and exceptional vessels reached 35ft, roughly double the draft of a top-rank paddle steamer of 1850.[7]

This is a familiar tale of woe, and steamships posed many other problems to the port authorities, including the need to undertake large and expensive dredging works and/or the construction of training walls. The purpose of this paper is the comparatively limited one of investigating the extent to which the successive new technologies of the paddle and the screw steamer made necessary the adoption of new technologies involving stationary or portable steam power in the construction and operation of the docks these vessels used.[8]

Hydraulic machinery

There are two respects in which the history of the adoption of hydraulic machinery has suffered from *post hoc, ergo propter hoc* reasoning, relating to two of its main applications. The first of these is that hydraulic lifting appliances were adopted because the high costs of steamship purchase and operation were justified chiefly by the ability to make more voyages per year. This, it is said, made it worth investing in expensive and innovative machinery in the interest of speed of turnround, particularly in discharge and to a lesser extent in loading. The larger and more accessible hatches of steamers removed an obvious constraint on those higher speeds. This would be an excellent argument, were it not for the intervention of some tiresome and disruptive facts. The first commercial use of hydraulic lifting appliances was at Albert Dock, Liverpool, a dock specifically built for sailing ships.[9]

Smith has argued that Liverpool was slow in moving into hydraulics and that this shows that the non-competitive nature of the operation of the port discouraged technical innovation. The fact is that hydraulic lifting appliances proliferated very rapidly at the enclosed warehouse docks, all of them geared to handling sailing ships, and scarcely at all anywhere else in the port. The reason for this is perfectly simple: at the warehouse docks, the dock workers were employees of the Port, in established jobs, eligible for various rudimentary welfare provision and paid a reasonable wage.[10] They were an expensive elite among dock workers, and it was worth investing in machinery to economise on their time. It was, in fact, where there *was* competition by independent master lumpers and porters in the discharging of ships that investment in hydraulic machines was small and where there was *no* competition it was large.[11] That is because the competition at the non-warehouse docks acted primarily on, and through the medium of, the greatly inferior wages and working conditions of casual workers.

There is an old maxim which says that 'An engineer is a man who can do for 10 shillings what any damn' fool can do for a pound'. The adoption of hydraulic lifting appliances, then, followed one of the basic rules of good engineering: innovate only where you need to, spend only where you need to, and let the rest look after itself according to existing best practice. Not only was it not driven by the arrival of the steamship, but in Liverpool it was almost solely provided for the discharge

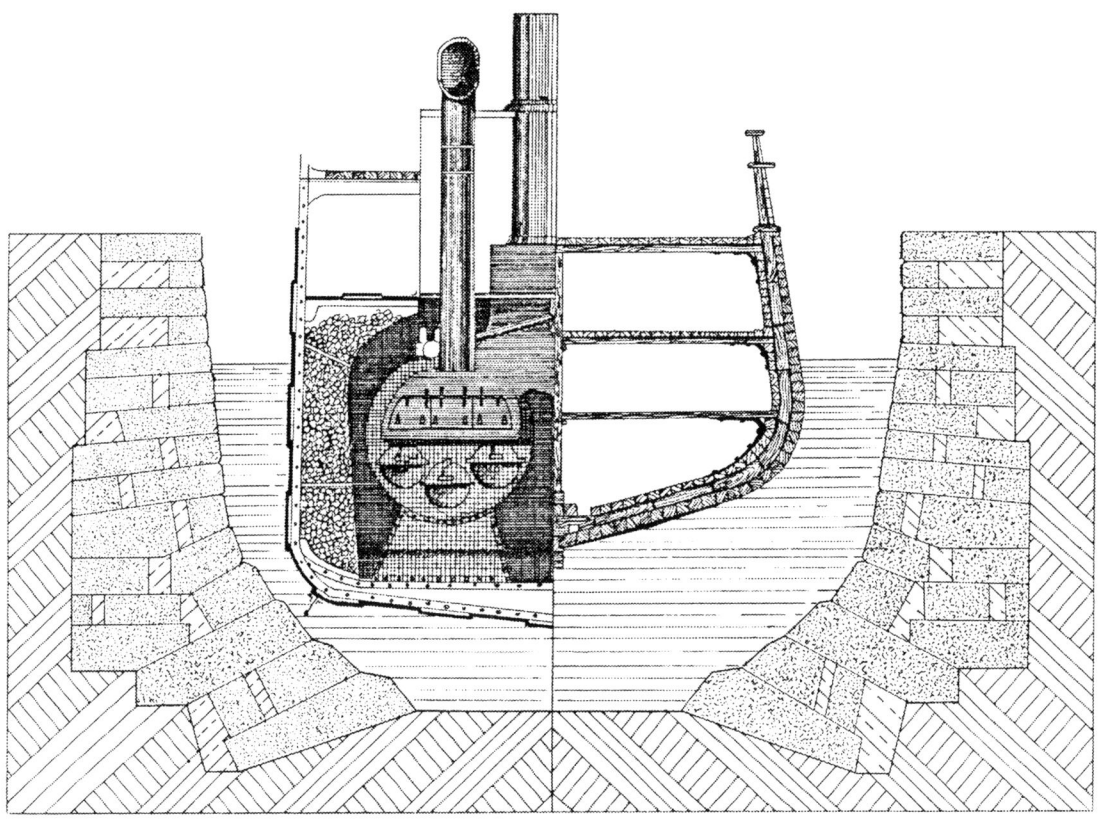

This composite drawing shows the comparative cross-sections of a typical sailing ship of about 1840, and a typical steamer of the same beam at the waterline dating from about 1880. It is obvious that the old passage of c1830 design would easily handle the sailing ship, but even a smallish steamer was working to very tight tolerances. Just one more reason why the steamship dictated massive port investment.

(and not loading) of sailing ships. The situation is exactly the reverse of what we have been led to expect.

Liverpool was, however, an atypical port in being very large, having a very diverse trade and yet still being owned and operated by a single authority. In London, hydraulic systems do indeed seem to have been adopted from the 1850s onwards primarily for loading and discharging goods at a wide variety of docks and wharves, and Smith lists 16 riverside wharves which were in the business in a big enough way to have their own pumping systems rather than merely buying power from someone else, in the years 1856-79. In those relatively early days, a river wharf (as distinct from a dock) would have little or no use for hydraulic power except for working lifting appliances.[12]

Railway-controlled ports were very enthusiastic about hydraulic systems, but here special circumstances applied. Most railway ports were involved to a greater or lesser extent in coal export, and hydraulic wagon-drops or specialist coaling cranes were a considerable improvement on balance tippers. Perhaps more significant was the railway companies' well-founded love of the hydraulic capstan: this cheap, simple and reliable device enabled two or three men to carry out a high proportion of the wagon movements on quaysides or in sidings without needing an expensive locomotive shunting up and down. In short, in railway ports as in Liverpool there is no necessary and logical connection between the arrival of steamships and the adoption of hydraulic handling equipment.

In some ports—Liverpool was one and Singapore another—quayside hydraulic cranes continued to find little favour with the engineers of steamship docks. The reason is quite simple: steamships, so far from increasing the demand for high-speed quayside lifting appliances actually diminished it by carrying perfectly sufficient lifting equipment—in the shape of steam deck winches and derricks—around with them. So effective was the use of ships' tackle that in most ports the problem was not how to get stuff out of a ship faster but how

to carry it away as fast as it could be got out. It was the porters, not the lumpers, who were the 'bottleneck'.[13] From about 1850, the largest sailing ships began to adopt the use of donkey boilers and steam winches in imitation of the steamers.

The second *post hoc* argument works the opposite way round, but is none the less wrong for that. In 1859, Jesse Hartley's huge Canada Entrance, 100ft wide, was opened. Each leaf of its gates weighed about 129 tons, and they were moved by hydraulic power.[14] Working a large entrance like that by hand took dozens of men, and, encouraged by a statement by G. P. Bidder that hydraulic gate motors saved the wages of about 40 men, the assumption has been made that gate motors were adopted to cut labour costs. In fact, unlike the lifting appliances, *they* genuinely were adopted to enhance the speed of turnround of those expensive paddle steamers for which Canada Entrance had been chiefly intended.

At a large entrance like Canada, the application of hydraulic power cut the time occupied by the actual operation of hand winches by around an hour, depending on the height of the tide and the weather conditions.[15] This considerably increased the ship-handling capacity per tide of the entrance, with a corresponding reduction in the risk of a vessel having to waste several hours (the exact number again depending on tide and weather) waiting for the next tide. It was another case of innovate where you have to and not elsewhere: at Canada there was a problem sufficient to justify the risks of installing a system new to the port.[16] That problem was not the payment of wages, but the pressure of vessels wanting to use the entrance during the brief period when the tide permitted a half-tide entrance to be left open or, in the case of a fully locked entrance, both inner and outer gates to be 'opened through'.

Large steamers made other new demands on dock facilities. Prior to about 1850, the movable bridges of the Dock Estate did not have to span passages wider than 50ft, so that hand-operated double-leaf swing bridges were adequate, if a little slow and laborious in operation. The rapid increase in passage widths made this traditional form impossibly large and heavy, necessitating the use of single leaf swing bridges, usually of bowstring girder or bar-stayed design. Such bridges could not be worked by hand at acceptable speed or cost: mechanical operation was virtually essential, and the form adopted was almost invariably hydraulic. There were exceptions to the adoption of swing bridges, but to the need for power operation there were very few. In the case of isolated installations, such as some of the swing bridges of the Manchester Ship Canal, the prime mover might be a gas engine, or later a heavy oil engine, but at earlier dates and within dock estates, steam ruled. These installations were not cheap: a typical movable bridge cost several thousand pounds exclusive of its power supply and its (extensive) foundation works.[17]

In the steam engine, often through the agency of hydraulic transmission, Victorian engineers enjoyed the ability to apply almost unlimited amounts of force or power to any difficulty they might face. In a few cases, the answer to the steamship's demand for faster attention to minor repairs was found not in the construction or alteration of graving docks, but in the installation of gigantic ship lifts. These devices depended on very simple reasoning: you want to get to the bottom of your ship? Easy, we'll lift it out of the water for you. The principle certainly was simple, but the scale of the equipment was vast. [18]

Hydraulic power stations came in many different shapes and sizes, but leaving aside the comparatively tiny single-purpose ones like those for a single isolated bridge, it was unusual to find one with an installed horsepower of under 100. More typical was one of 300-400 hp, supplied by three boilers if they were very large ones, more likely by four or five moderately large ones.[19] These boilers never stopped: because so many things depended on the hydraulic system, the pressure had to be kept up in the system 365 days a year. Even when no power was being drawn, one engine would have to run a little from time to time to make up

the 'standing losses', for even in a high quality system in a good state of repair there was always a little leakage somewhere. As the systems got older, the standing losses increased. Actual coal consumption figures are hard to find, just the occasional odd logbook having survived, but a medium-to-large size installation seems typically to have burned around 2,000-3,000 tons per year.[20]

Screw steamers, Graving Docks and Enormous Pumps

In the early days of the screw steamer, visits to graving docks were very frequent. Troubles with propellors and shafts were far from unknown, and we even find the 'Edwardian Floating Palaces' having such troubles: *Mauretania* more than once arrived in port with only three screws. Long-haul vessels passing through the tropics before the development of effective anti-fouling paints often needed a quick scrape and a paint every voyage to regain their design speed and, more particularly, fuel consumption. The trouble with screw steamers, especially passenger steamers, was not just that they were typically deeper than sailing ships, but that they were proportionately more deeper when unladen, for the obvious reason that their engines and boilers were still aboard. Major ports were also expected to consider the possible demands of visiting warships, and ironclad steamers could shed even less of their draft than could passenger liners. This meant that even if the wet docks of a port could accommodate the deeper vessels, the graving docks, which had traditionally been built shallower because they only had to take unladen vessels, possibly could not.[21]

This problem had been becoming acute in Liverpool from the 1860s onwards. It was never publicly admitted by the Board, though much discussed within it, that the provision of graving docks was unprofitable: they were seen chiefly as a service to customers whose money was spent in the wet docks. As a result, from the 1860s onwards, we find periodic complaints about the graving docks not being deep enough.

Particularly unsatisfactory were the large Langton Graving Docks, specifically built to house the largest class of steamer, which proved insufficiently deep by 1886, just four years after they opened.[22] A great oppportunity had also been missed at the other end of the estate, where the entrances and basin of Herculaneum Dock had been substantially deepened at great expense, but the sills of the graving docks opening off it had not.[23]

The situation had a political dimension as well. It was not until 1888 that the Board completed the massive programme of works enabled under the 1873 Dock Act. If the Board were to seek to close docks and borrow further large amounts of money in order to deepen the graving docks, they would require a further Act, and one can well imagine the joy with which Counsel for objectors would have pounced on such a Bill in its Committee stages. The Board had come under heavy criticism during the epic contests over the Manchester Ship Canal Bills, and faced frequent objections to a number of Bills of its own around this time.[24] A solution to the graving dock problem which did not require going to Parliament would have considerable attractions.

It did not take a genius, which was just as well, since their Engineer-in-Chief was not one, to work out that if the distance between the top and the bottom of the water was insufficient and you could not conveniently lower the bottom, you might be able to raise the top. The depths at the graving docks were mostly sufficient during spring tides, but during neaps the level in the impounded docks off which the graving docks opened could fall, over the course of a week, by several feet, exceptionally as much as 11ft. If the level could be maintained at or even a little above HWST by pumping, all would be fairly well. The obvious place to start was Herculaneum, for the hydraulic 'bucketing engine' which Armstrong's had supplied for draining the graving docks there had been a disaster and had been replaced with an old locomotive cobbled up to drive chain pumps.[25] Working closely with the famous pump-makers J & H Gwynne of Hammersmith, Lyster came up with a scheme for a dual-purpose pumping installation which would vastly enhance the rate of emptying the graving docks and which could also impound water from the river. The total cost was estimated at £26,000, but the scheme proved extremely controversial within the Board, and was eventually shelved.

What went ahead instead was a broadly similar dual-purpose station at Sandon Dock, authorised by the Board at an estimated cost of £23,000 on 17 January 1884. It took two years to build, and was overspent by some £6,000. Among the 'extras' which were brought forth to justify this were the installation of a fourth boiler, so that one boiler could be down for maintenance without stopping the job, and an overhead gantry in the pumphouse for maintenance purposes.[26] These were not, course, 'extras' at all, but essential parts of accepted prudent engineering practice which it would have been both unusual and foolish to omit. The station worked successfully, however, and was soon followed by others at Coburg, Wallasey and Huskisson Docks. Each of these was larger than the pilot scheme at Sandon, but all were equipped by Gwynne's.

At this point we must pause and consider the immensity of what the Board had taken on. They intended to raise the level of Sandon Dock by five feet by pumping for about three hours over high water. One inch of water over the area of 1 acre is approximately 22,400 gallons, or 100 tons. There were four pumps, which delivered water at the rate of 685.6 tons per minute, some 38,395 gallons per minute from each pump.[27] In this first, rather experimental set-up, simple-expansion steam engines were used, and one source suggests that they may have exhausted straight to atmosphere, innocent of a condenser. In the hour and a half the engines ran on their first full-scale trial, they consumed 3,808 lbs of coal—but in that time they performed the amount of work for which the specification allowed three hours. One main pump also succeeded in pumping out one of the graving docks in 38 minutes.

This impressive performance underlines the rapid progress made in the design of centrifugal pumps, which were found to be ideally suited to the movement of large volumes of silty water through a relatively small lift. Having no valves which could stick or suffer damage, the centrifugal pump's high flow velocity also minimised the risk of clogging up. Effective centrifugal pumps had appeared in America by 1820, but the first successful examples in Britain were probably those shown at the Great Exhibition,[28] and the first practical dock installation in Britain seems to have been a relatively small (25 hp) machine employed at Swansea in 1861 for making good lockage losses. Grimsby and Leith in 1863 and Marseilles the following year came close behind, all of these installations for draining graving docks.[29] There was still some trial and error going on: the Marseilles installation used brass rotors, which suffered from severe 'galvanic action' and had to be replaced with cast iron ones. Above all, the early examples were tiny: that at Great Grimsby, for example, lifted only 3,600 gpm.

In London, impounding had been tried at a very early date for a completely different reason from that which applied in Liverpool: lockage and leakage water had to be made good, and the obvious way to do this was by letting in water at high tide, but this caused rapid silt deposition and resulted in high dredging costs. (Sir) John Rennie had the idea that pumping from the river, from near surface level, where the water was less disturbed and thus bore a smaller silt burden, would solve the problem, and installed pumps between 1828 and 1830. They were abandoned as a failure in 1843, suggesting that before centrifugal pumps were available, impounding was not a sound or practical proposition.[30]

There was, in theory, a much simpler way, namely the scoop-wheel, and this was the solution adopted at Millwall Docks as late as 1885: two wheels, of 32ft and 36ft diameter were driven by two steam engines of 360 hp, lifting about 30,000 tons per hour. This installation 'fell out of use' at an unknown

date, but was not scrapped until 1920. John Gwynne, leading manufacturer of centrifugal pumps, was understandably scornful:

There are a few engineers and others who have a lingering belief in scoop wheels… Just as the [water] turbine has supplanted the overshot and breast wheels—both fairly efficient machines—so must the centrifugal engine suspersede the scoop wheel.[31]

The Royal Albert Docks (London) had already introduced centrifugal impounding pumps, and they seem to have been less efficient than the Liverpool ones, even though they were driven by compound condensing engines, which should have more than compensated for any efficiency gains achieved by continued development of the pumps. They were considerably smaller than the Sandon pumps, having a maximum total delivery of 23,600 tons/hr compared with 40,000 at Sandon.[32]

While we may question the wisdom of the Sandon scheme, there is no doubt it did the job. It was a successful 'cheap fix' in the short term, for it solved the graving docks problem without undue embarrassment and it had the substantial additional advantage of allowing some of the older and obsolescent docks to handle deeper ships, pending the time when they could be fully and properly modernised. Kings and Queens in particular were fairly large and spacious docks sadly deficient in depth which were given a new lease of life by the Coburg station.[33] But the impounding approach had its problems: in Birkenhead, the impounded water area was no less than 160 acres, needing 16,000 tons of water to raise the level an inch. The stations at Wallasey, Coburg and Huskisson Docks were of larger capacity than that at Sandon, those at Coburg lifting up to 1,200 tons/minute, and the pumps were of a more sophisticated design, being direct-driven from the crankshafts of vertical tandem compound steam engines.[34] This mind-bending amount of water can perhaps best be appreciated by equating it with the combined output of about 300 large modern fire engines.

But cheap fixes are bound to have

disadvantages. There were extensive coaling facilities at Birkenhead, and more than one complaint was made that the sterling efforts of the chaps in the impounding station, perhaps to get a large vessel into graving dock, made it impossible for a lofty unladen ship to get under the coal drops. Above all, however, it was a saving of capital at the expense of the revenue albatross of keeping a total of about 15 Lancashire boilers in steam all the time. That took about 6,000 tons of coal per station per year and the wages of the people to shovel it.[35] In the early days of the installations, coal cost about 8 shillings per ton, so the cost of coal alone would have paid the interest costs on a debt in the region of £240,000—a sum which, added to the £100,000+ which the stations had cost, would have made a more-than-useful start on

deepening a graving dock or two, since the two Langton Graving docks had cost less than that to construct from scratch. Wallasey Dock impounding station had a complement of 21 full-time and seven part-time employees, and the others presumably had about the same, making a total of around 100. There were also two significant maintenance costs: those of the machinery itself and those of the additional dredging made necessary by the silt brought in by the pumps. Wallasey Dock, some 12 $^3/_4$ acres of water space, was eventually abandoned as a full-time sediment chamber. At Coburg, the dredging cost in 1889, the last year before pumping started, was £228 and in 1905 it was £2365: in 1908 pumping ceased and the dredging cost fell to £589. The repairs and maintenance cost of the pumping plant was

Excavations at Gladstone Dock in 1922. This view conveys something of the scale of works rendered necessary by the constant pressure exerted by ship-owners on port authorities.

£3,689, which in relation to first cost was a little above average for the general run of steam plant.

There is, of course, one major item thus far unconsidered, which is the cost in lost revenue of closing parts of the dock system for major works. So far as can be told, the Board never attempted to work out this indirect cost of modernisation or construction works, though it was obviously well aware of its existence. The Engineer's estimates never adopted the railway practice of including a notional sum for 'possession'.[36]

Some consideration was given above to pumping out graving docks. Ports like Liverpool and Bristol, with a large tidal variation, were long able to drain their graving docks simply by pulling out the plug on a falling tide. Starting in ports which did not enjoy large variations, the use of pumps spread rapidly to others. Initially they were very modest machines: the installation at Clarence graving docks, for example, consumed only a little over one ton of coal per week.[37] The graving dock pumps in large new works eventually achieved a size almost equalling that of the impounding pumps: the new ones at Canada Graving Dock, for example, were installed in 1899 at a cost of £20,727. There were three of them, with 51 inch suctions, as compared with 60 inch at the larger impounding stations, and they were supplied by eight Babcock boilers costing a further £4,980.[38]

Gladstone Graving Dock was pumped out by the Board's first major Diesel engine installation at the rate of 350,000 gpm, requiring 4,000 bhp. The need for these increased rates of delivery was only partly a question of turnround time: as the docks got bigger and deeper the amount of water left in them at the bottom of the tide increased, so it became necessary to be able to pump fast enough to ensure that the dock was empty before the tide started to rise again. The time taken varied enormously from dock to dock, not just with size but according to the design skills applied and the quality of the machinery, but anything over four hours was considered pretty poor, and mighty installations like those at Canada and Gladstone aimed to do it in around 2-2 $\frac{1}{2}$ hours. 'It', in the case of Gladstone, was about 44 million gallons, varying according to the size of the ship.[39]

One may note in passing that the considerable cost of pumping posed an interesting dilemma as to how to charge for the use of graving docks. The larger the ship in relation to the dock, the more time and effort was required to position and shore her. On the other hand, the smaller the vessel, the less water she displaced before the gates were shut, and therefore the more pumping was necessary. Port authorities seem always to have charged more for large ships than for small, but this was probably more a question of 'what the market will bear' than a reflection of the actual costs.

Steam plant for dock construction

The earliest use of steam power in construction work dates from well before the days of the steamship: John Rennie (Snr) used two Boulton & Watt engines for spoil raising at the West India Docks from 1801, and John Foster, acting on Rennie's advice, did likewise at Princes Dock Liverpool from 1811.[40] In both cases, the stimulus to innovation was the shortage of men and horses occasioned by war with France. In more normal circumstances, the horse-drawn barrow-run was still a cheap and effective method. What changed that was the ever-greater depths from which spoil had to be lifted, necessitating the adoption not only of winding engines, but of locomotive-hauled inclines and of steam 'travellers'. It was generally considered that the cost of excavation and masonrywork varied roughly as the cube of the depth to which it was necessary to work.[41]

The most acute problem in going deeper, however, was water. The simple but essential task of keeping the major part of the workings dry became ever more complex and expensive the deeper the engineer's men dug. The Somerset [Graving] Dock at Malta provides a fine example: they dug a pump well, as one should, right at the beginning of work and at 6ft below sea level it struck water: at 17ft it did so again and at 43ft, again. At a depth of 25ft

300gpm of water needed removing, while at the necessary depth of 43ft it was 5,725gpm. The result was that in a fairly large but technically comparatively simple scheme costing a total of £150,000, the staggering sum of £20,000 was spent on coal for the pumps — and £1,600 on lubricating oil. The last 23% of depth accounted for 94% of the pumping costs and 12% of the total cost of the dock was spent on coal.[42] Any half-decent dock extension programme counted its coal costs in thousands of tons per year, and the largest single consumer was normally the pumps.

The next largest user was the assorted cranes, travellers, derricks etc, most of whose horsepower was exerted in spoil removal. Most, but not all, for as the works got deeper so the retaining walls got higher. They had, of course, to get higher from the bottom rather than from the top, and the base thickness was anything from twice to four times that at the coping. Going down 33ft instead of 30ft did not increase the weight of masonry by 10% but by at least 20%.[43] Similar proportions applied to large temporary works such as cofferdams, with the result that the power needs for material handling—thousands of tons of stone, mortar and timber—rose rapidly. Finally, a relatively small and esoteric use of steam power was the arrival of electric floodlighting. This was pioneered in Liverpool in the late 1870s, and was made necessary by the fact that increased depth of working made the available time for tidal working much shorter, so it became worth burning yet more coal in order to be able to gain the maximum benefit from low tides in hours of darkness.[44]

Of course it was possible to dig docks deeper without using ever-greater amounts of steam power. It was, however, so difficult, dangerous and expensive that few engineers would consider it an option. It is important to remember that although provision of coal, oil and water for the machinery sounds at first hearing like revenue expenditure, it was invariably charged to the capital costs of construction, which were normally paid for with borrowed money, so that when port authorities were agonising about their debt charges in the early part of the twentieth century, one little bit of their problem stemmed from the burning of large amounts of coal perhaps twenty years before.

One area in which it is easy to over-estimate the importance of steam ashore is that of excavation. Steam navvies, and more particularly land dredgers, could be strikingly successful in certain circumstances. A Boulet land dredger employed on the Manchester Ship Canal shifted 2,000 cu yd/day, but the same machine had previously been employed at Canada No 2 Branch in Liverpool. There the varying nature of the ground, the constricted layout of the site and the number of corners needing to be dug out restricted its output to a maximum of 770 cu yd/day. Its performance could thus be roughly equated with that of 100 first class navvies shovelling into railway wagons—and it needed 40 men to keep it moving on its temporary roadway and supplied with spoil wagons. It also required fairly frequent repair.[45] The experiment was not repeated in Liverpool, though steam navvies continued to be used when appropriate. In general, dock works were too fiddly and complex to provide much scope for machines which were highly useful in canal, railway and road building.

The Direct Connection: Bunker Coal

The supply of bunker coal posed no difficulties in those ports which already had significant coal export trades, or which were located very close to one which did. A number of the larger general ports, including London, Liverpool and Bristol, did not, and of these only Liverpool was sufficiently conveniently connected to major coalfields to cause any great puzzlement among the Trustees, later the Members of the Board, as to their overall policy on coal. Coal was a low-value trade, but it was steady and it could manage with, by Liverpool's standards, second-rate dock accommodation. In times of recession, shipowners could be glad of an export cargo of coal because it was more profitable than sailing in ballast, though only marginally so if you were not a specialist in the trade. It was necessary to decide whether coal handling was purely a service to steamship owners or whether it was a traffic of the port as well. In London, despite the absence of any unitary port authority, the provision of bunker coal was unanimously left to contractors, and London was, of course, an importer rather than exporter of coal.[46] In Liverpool, the normal decisiveness of the Trustees deserted them: when Jesse Hartley provided them with a scheme for a high-level coal railway to handle both cargo and bunker coal they accepted it in principle but authorised him to build only about two thirds of what he had designed. It proved to be the beginning of a very long-standing headache. The wagon cranes required a considerable horsepower of hydraulic machinery and by 1890 the railway was consuming about 1,000 tons of coal per year to handle, typically, something approaching 500,000 tons per year.[47] It is difficult to generalise, because the relative prices of coal from different sources of supply varied, causing demand for particular grades to vary as well, but very roughly one third of that seems to have gone into bunkers, two thirds into holds.[48]

It is highly doubtful whether the high-level coal railway ever met its true costs.[49] If it did, then it was probably, with a nice irony, only when passenger liners became too large to coal in dock at all. The Edwardian express liners used up to 5,000 tons per voyage, and they were coaled in the river by the Liverpool Barge & Coal Company, using barges and floating elevators. These could conveniently use Bramley-Moore, which was by now entirely outgrown by even modest ocean-going vessels, and therefore readily available for the frenzied comings and goings of barges to coal the Atlantic greyhounds.[50] If one were able to add in the administrative costs of the endless disputes with the Lancashire & Yorkshire Railway, it must surely have lost money. Like the graving docks, it represented a lot of expensive machinery built and operated as a loss-leader to tempt steamship owners to use Liverpool.

Conclusion

By getting first wider and then deeper, steamships posed intractable problems for dock engineers and their paymasters. Their response was to enlist the aid of some important new technologies which were emerging in other fields and adapt them to their purposes. Their particular contribution was the very large scale of much of the machinery. The bulk grain handling machinery at Waterloo Dock, Liverpool, had an hydraulic station of 360hp in 1868—enormous for that date—and the larger impounding stations and graving dock pumps in any port that used them came to pack several hundred horsepower, the biggest by the end of the century running into thousands.

This may be thought to typify the attitude of at least one substantial school of late nineteenth century engineering: boundless faith in sheer size and horsepower. The problem of building a bridge close to the Tower of London could be met by the brutally simple expedient of heaving some 3,000 tons of metal about by hydraulic power. When dock gates got too big to be worked by hand, hydraulics could apply almost any desired amount of force. Ships came to need very heavy items (like spare engines or boilers) handled at graving docks and a 100-ton hydraulic crane was the answer.

The reason, of course, that ships were ever more demanding can be linked to exactly the same attitude: the desire for higher carrying power in ships set builders and owners into a spiral of increasing size and power. It might be foolhardy to suggest that a numerical relationship could be discovered, and some of the causes and effects are certainly not simple matters of technological determinism. On the other hand, a more general statement that continuing and accelerating increases in horsepower afloat demanded approximately parallel increases in horsepower ashore seems eminently defensible.

Think Big? Returns on different scales of investment in the Port of Liverpool 1873-1905.[51]

It was Gordon jackson who, in his seminal *History and Archaeology of British Ports*, first called into question the idea that the changes in ships and trade during the late nineteenth century made it essential for port authorities to make large and repeated investments in ever-larger facilities. Some, such as Hyde, had virtually used such investment as an indicator of the success of a port in keeping abreast of the times.

Jackson, working from aggregated national figures, drew attention to a situation where where curves of port investment and tonnage handled ran roughly parallel but with a time lag of five or six years apparently corresponding to the time required for design and construction.[52] He observed that after about 1880, the return ceased to increase as rapidly as the investment. The present writer took up this theme using traditional narrative sources to suggest that shipowners' expectations of port authorities were out of all proportion to their willingness to pay port charges at levels which would even meet the interest cost of the infrastructure, much less provide for the rapid depreciation brought about by their own activities.[53] In extreme cases, shipping companies were found giving 'indications' that investment in, say, Fishguard or Milford Haven[54] would earn large returns when in fact all they wanted was competitive sticks with which to beat the established liner ports for better facilities or lower dues.

This paper seeks to draw the two themes together in the context of investment in the Port of Liverpool. It will be seen that Jackson's approach can be justified at two levels of disaggregation, by first using figures for Liverpool only and then going to the level of individual docks only. However, although the narrative of engineering work at any particular dock can be long and complex, and can normally be traced in considerable detail, it does not necessarily provide what we actually need to know to assess the worth of the investment. To achieve that we need to look at that dock in the context both of its immediate neighbours and of the port as a whole.

The solution adopted here is to analyse the investment in, and the revenue from, four groups of docks where major work was undertaken as a specific and finite project. This eliminates the uncertainties which would be encountered by following a single dock over time (eg. in distinguishing between maintenance and improvement) or by studying a running theme such as the installation of electric cranes. In effect it breaks the paper into four case studies, representing four different kinds of project.

The works under the Liverpool Docks Extension Act of 1873 formed the largest and most expensive programme undertaken in the port to that time, at a total estimated cost of £4.1 million. By far the greater part of their water area was completely 'new build'.[55] They have here been divided into North and South works, because the two groups were built with two separate markets in view. The North Works were very specifically stated to be for serving the largest vessels afloat,[56] while the South Works were intended for the medium-to-large long-haul cargo liners. They have, therefore, been treated separately in the hope that their relative effectiveness as investments might cast some light on the old controversy referred to below.

The works under the 1891 Dock Act represent the main alternative approach, of carrying out heavy modernisation works on existing facilities, placing the emphasis more on enhanced ship-handling capacity rather than on extension of the area of the docks: it is chiefly an efficiency-geared project. While this may appear a more sophisticated engineering approach it has the potential disadvantage of causing even greater disruption to trade while the work is in hand, and there is always the risk on 'brown field sites' of encountering unpleasant and expensive surprises underground.

The final project studied, the Queens Dock improvements, did not require Parliamentary authority and although capital in nature, was funded from revenue. This scheme, as emerges below, is the only clear case of the quantitative methods used here suggesting a significantly different conclusion from that previously drawn, or at least suspected, by qualitative methods. The major surprise comes not in any one of the projects but in the relationship between them.

A Note on Sources

The published *Annual Accounts* give details of the Board's borrowing and of the major items of expenditure (as well as many minor ones), and they include a running table each year giving the tonnage of shipping and revenue earnings of the docks from 1751 to the year in question. Graphs of these figures are derived from the author's Excel files. Figures for individual docks come from the *Annual*

Revenue Statements which survive from 1844-1924 and were keyed into Excel by Graham Tonks, a research assistant funded by the University of Liverpool. Where it is obvious from which of these sources figures quoted are derived, they have not been individually referenced. Narrative and description of the work carried out is, unless otherwise stated, derived from the published annual *Report of the Engineer*.

The North Works under the Liverpool Docks Extension Act, 1873

Investment began in financial year 1873-74[57] with the expenditure of £33,078. Although the greater part of the total expenditure was incurred before the royal opening of Alexandra Dock in 1881, fairly large sums continued to be spent until the completion of Hornby Dock (nominally in 1884), ending with £58,210 in 1885, which made a total for the project to that point of £2,513,164. The last payments under the Act were of £4,721 in 1899, but unfortunately by that time the expenditure is no longer itemised in the accounts, so we do not know exactly where that money was spent.

Of the new-build docks, Alexandra was an almost immediate success in terms of tonnage handled. Formally opened in 1881, in 1883 it

East Side, Coburg Dock, in 1891. The buildings nearest the quay were, like the equivalents at Queens, demolished as part of the improvement programme. The present line of the Dock Road is marked by the next street inland.

handled 1,631,525 tons of shipping and earned £247,589 in dues, both of which were by far the largest figures for a single dock in the port. It was admittedly the largest single dock in terms of water area, but in 1890 it was also top dock in terms of both tonnage and revenue per yard of quay with figures of 537.1 tons and £76 respectively.[58] However, the figures for the other new docks in the programme were somewhat disappointing. Langton was best of the rest with £48.8 and 330 tons, but Hornby could scarcely be considered a great success with £15.7 and 106.6 tons.

We may compare these figures with some for older docks. Nelson Dock, for example, was opened in 1848 for the then largest vessels using the port, but by 1890 it had 'gravitated' and was engaged mainly in European trades, with some of the larger coastwise traders using it as well. It was earning a very respectable £43.2 per yard on traffic of 407 tons per yard. It had received no significant modernisation since its opening, but Princes Dock, opened in 1821 had gone without for even longer and with £22.2 and 172 tons it still easily outperformed Hornby.

It would be tempting to explain the relatively poor performance of Langton and Hornby in terms of the well-known weaknesses of the re-designing of Canada Entrance as part of the same programme, and in 1890 G. F. Lyster, the Engineer-in-Chief, was about to make another attempt to satisfy the customers with yet further alterations to the entrance. This was clearly not the only problem, though, because access to Alexandra was via the same entrance which served Langton and Hornby.

Another way of appraising this programme is by looking at the strategic level. It had cost, in round figures, £2,500,000, at a time when the total capital debt of the Board was £16,805,585, so its cost was approximately 15% of the Board's total debt. Did it earn its money? Between 1883 and 1887 the total dues revenue of the Board *fell,* but was this chiefly due to cuts in the rates of dues made in 1884? Only in part, for the total shipping tonnage handled

exhibits a slight, steady growth between 1881 and 1884 followed by a decline to a low point in 1887 and then another gentle and steady rise to a peak in 1892. There is no discontinuity which one might reasonably attribute to the very large investment made. Because the borrowing was unmatched by a consequent large increase in revenue, the proportion of the Board's dues income which went to pay interest rose again. It had been at very high levels in the late 1860s, briefly crossing the 100% mark in 1867,[59] but declined sharply between 1869 and 1878 before beginning to rise again. Unfortunately our sequence of figures becomes broken at 1880—a crucial date for present purposes—by the Board's change in borrowing policy: they increasingly moved to selling annuities and issuing promissory notes as alternatives to the old method of raising funds entirely as bond debts. After an initial fluctuation, the new method shows us a steady climb to a 20-year high of 78% in 1886 followed by a gratifying decline which lasted until 1892. This, sadly, was not brought about by a rise in income resulting from the new docks but by a fall in the rate of interest, and when rates rose again after 1900, so did the percentage.

There are well-known dangers in the use of volume rather than values, but the most perfunctory examination of tonnage figures appears to offer strong confirmation of the misgivings expressed above. Between 1873 and 1880, total tonnage using the port grew from 6,574,742 to 7,524,533: in the latter year none of the new docks under the Act had opened and the Estate was obstructed by literally thousands of men with shovels. Between 1880 and 1883, tonnage rose by almost exactly one million—including the supposed 1.5 million contributed by the newly-opened Alexandra and the quadrupling of Langton's tonnage (as a result of completion of the river entrance) to nearing half a million!

What was happening? Alexandra's tonnage and revenue both rocketed up over the two years 1881-83 and then levelled off, which is no doubt what the Board and their engineer hoped and expected would happen. But the reason why the overall tonnage and revenue of the Board showed little increase with the opening of Alexandra is made clear by the graphs showing Alexandra's tonnage and revenue as percentages of the totals for the port: they show very similar shapes, indicating that Alexandra's impressive traffic was won not through growth in international trade, nor from other competing ports, but from other docks within the Port of Liverpool. Worse, Alexandra's 'market share' within the port does not show a downward trend until its tonnage and revenue do, that is to say that it did was not providing excess capacity which gradually got taken up through growth of trade over the years. When it finally does show a definite fall, it is accompanied by an equally definite fall in both tonnage and revenue— which are accounted for by the completion of the Canada-Huskisson scheme considered below.

In short, it appears that the new north docks built under the 1873 Dock Extension Act did not make any radical improvement in the trade of the port, and certainly nothing approaching the 15% increase which they brought about in its debt. Nor did they earn enough to pay the interest on that new debt. The Board's bonds at any one time always bore various rates of interests, fixed at the time of purchase, but the new bonds being issued in the late 1870s averaged out at about 4%, an interest cost on the project of marginally over £100,000 per year. Clearly Alexandra alone far more than covered that, but as we have seen, Alexandra's apparently impressive income arose chiefly from vessels moving there from other docks: it certainly does not represent new income which, as we have seen, was not being generated. Part of the cause of the migration is probably quite simple: traffic was shifting around within the port trying to avoid the Engineer and all his works, and once he had gone to make a mess somewhere else, the customers could get back to business as normal—squabbling among themselves and with the Board for occupancy of the best berths. We must remember that, with all its

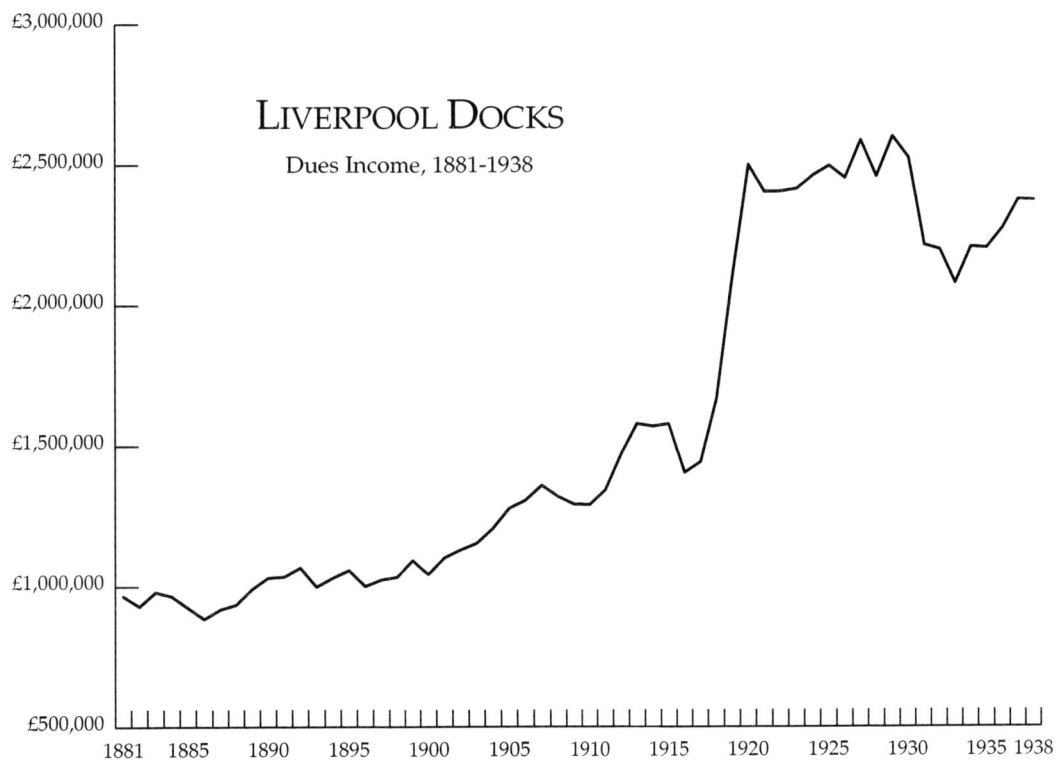

LIVERPOOL DOCKS

Dues Income, 1881-1938

problems, Alexandra when first opened *did* provide the best berths: it is just that they were still not good enough.

Next we must enquire whether this mediocre performance was because the general state of trade was poor, and we find that, apart from the occasional fluctuation, the total tonnage of shipping entering British ports rose consistently during the early life of these new docks.[60] Jackson has pointed out the need to beware of such aggregate figures because they can mask misleading factors like the very rapid growth of the British coal export trade. One of the factors they mask here is the boom in the emigration trade brought about by the agricultural depression—a trade in which Liverpool predominated at that date and which employed large ships of exactly the kind for which the new north docks had been

designed. Coupled with the agricultural depression was the high level of food importing, especially grain from Russia and USA. While Russian grain would go mainly to London and Hull, Liverpool took the lion's share of US wheat. The US cotton import trade fluctuated, but on average increased over the decade. In short, it seems that looking at the aggregate figures is unlikely to provide any major statistical pitfall, and that some at least of Liverpool's traditional major trades were not suffering but benefiting from conditions in the wider economic world. Rather as the diversity of Liverpool's trade had enabled it to ride out the recurrent financial crises earlier in the century with comparative ease, so now it secured it against 'depression'.[61]

Finally, it must be asked whether these figures conceal the new docks suffering from

Heavy reconstruction works: this view is actually of the reconstruction of West Trafalgar in about 1930. The availability of the Salisbury clock tower as a vantage point for the photographer enablea a very clear impression of the way modernisation works could be more complex than 'new build'.

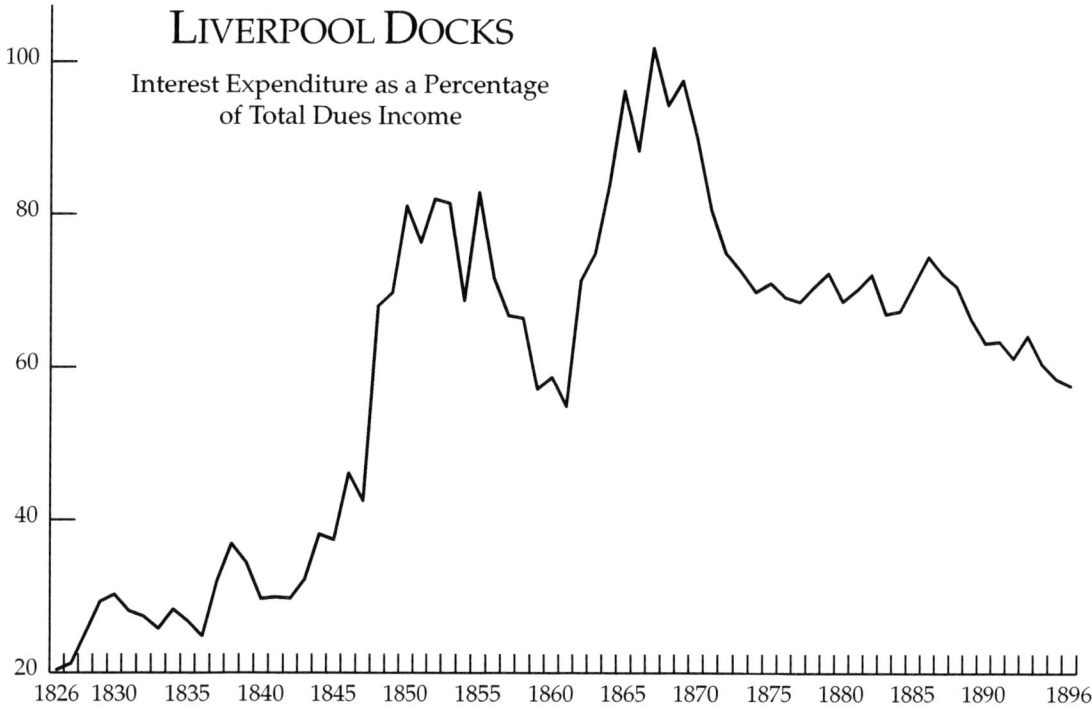

LIVERPOOL DOCKS

Interest Expenditure as a Percentage
of Total Dues Income

teething problems, whether in their design or construction or through an initial customer resistance to their being so far away from the city centre. The sad fact is that they did not really come good later: Alexandra, for example, earned its peak revenue as early as 1889 and it was downhill all the way from there: in 1913 it earned £153,518 as compared with £247,589 in 1883, the first year in which it was not seriously affected by engineering works in the adjoining docks, and, more particularly by the fact that the work of deepening the Canada Entrance was at last completed—or at least that particular deepening was. Hornby, starting from a lower base, did improve significantly, peaking at £120,776 in 1899. After only 15 years, it too was on the slide. The only obvious way of testing the 'distance hypothesis' is by comparing trade immediately before and after the opening of the Liverpool Overhead Railway made business access to the city much easier, and in 1894, the first full year's working after the railway opened, Alexandra exhibited a slight *fall* in both tonnage and revenue.

This re-opens the issue argued so vehemently at the time: was investment aimed at exceptional ships a sensible option? Since the average-size ships formed the majority of the customers, docks for the exceptional ships were only a rational choice if, as their advocates claimed, they could profitably be handed down to other trades when they were superseded. It appears that in this case they could be handed down, but not profitably in terms of dues. If we look at the tonnage figures instead we can really see the failure of that argument, because the average cargo-liner had a much higher NRT:GRT ratio than the north Atlantic passenger liners: the substitution of the one for the other in a particular dock ought to result in a *more* than proportionate rise in tonnage, and it did not. On the contrary: when completion of the new Sandon Entrances resulted in the largest passenger liners moving to Canada/Huskisson, tonnage there rose extremely rapidly while at Alexandra, where they had been before, it *fell* from 1,656,193 in 1902 to 1,616,494 in 1903, and this at a time when the Board's total tonnage was growing strongly.

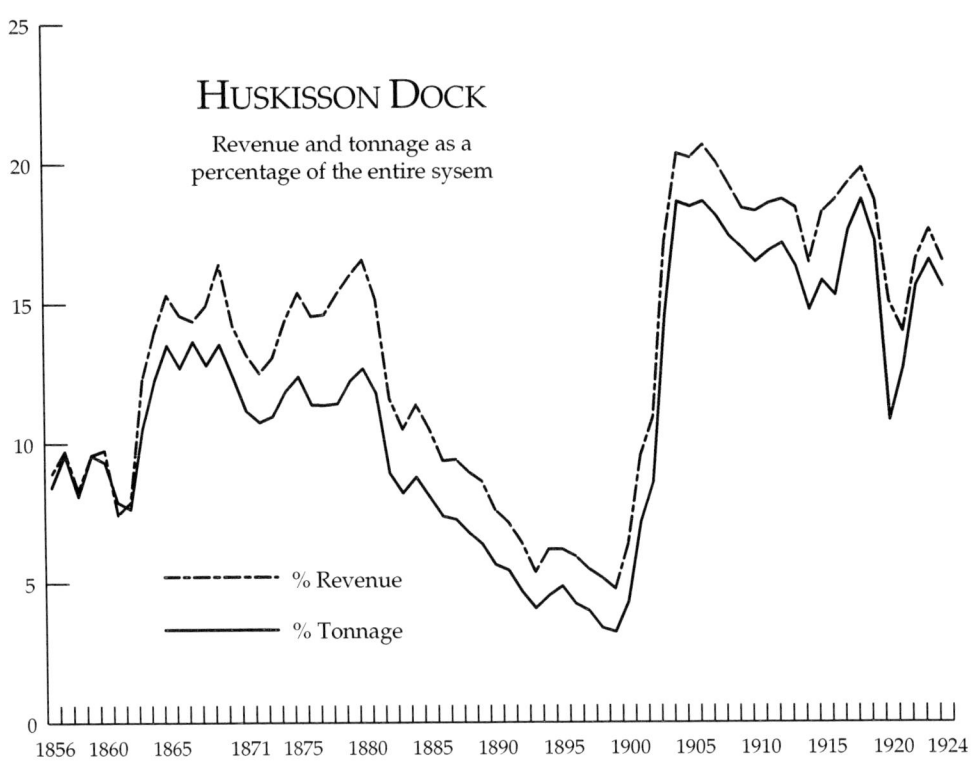

HUSKISSON DOCK

Revenue and tonnage as a
percentage of the entire sysem

- - - - % Revenue
——— % Tonnage

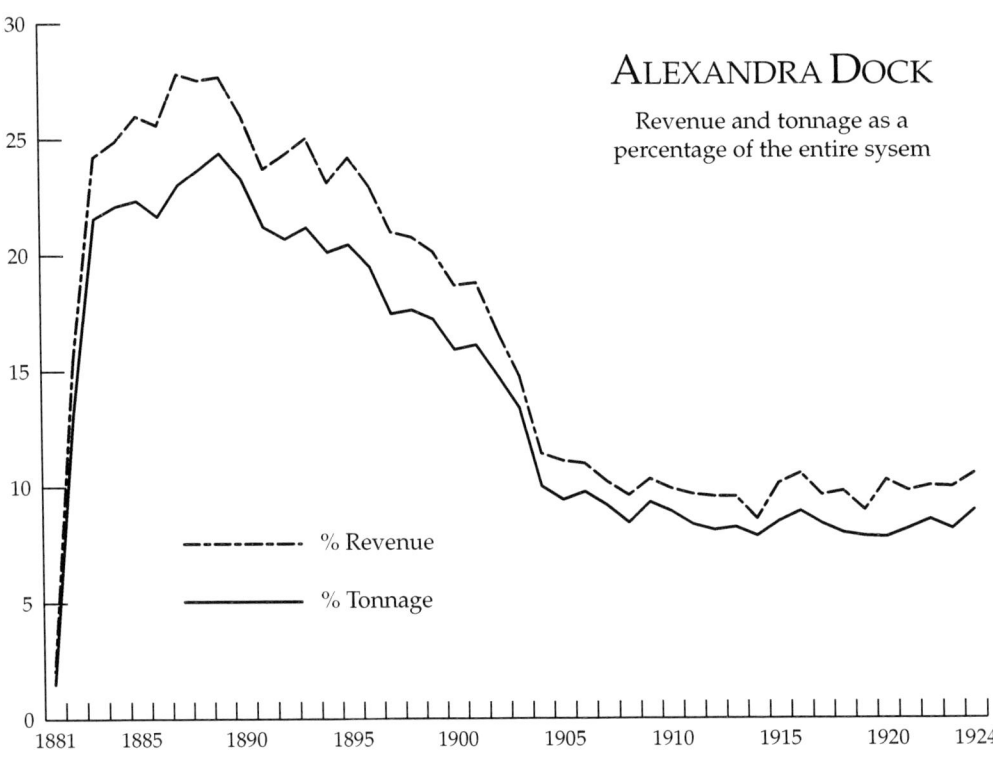

ALEXANDRA DOCK

Revenue and tonnage as a
percentage of the entire sysem

- - - - % Revenue
——— % Tonnage

This, of course, bears out in quantitative terms what I long ago suggested in qualitative ones namely that the Board failed, through its Works Committee, to provide the Engineer with a carefully thought-out brief as to what was needed and then ensure that he executed it correctly.[62] It really can be stated as simply as that, because for present purposes it does not matter at what stage in the process the engineering went wrong, or whose fault it might have been. The North Works under the 1873 Act were not good enough, either new for exceptional ships or secondhand for average ones. They did not win sufficient new traffic to pay for themselves, and they did not do the job for which they were designed, making further heavy expenditure necessary within less than a decade.

The New South Works under the 1873 Act

This was not nearly such a large project, and in 1890 when its expenditure ceased to appear separately in the accounts the total spent to date was £1,342,293. It was qualitatively as well as quantitatively different from the north works. Unlike them , the aim was not to accommodate the largest vessels using the port, but those often regarded as its bread and butter, operated by well-known cargo-liner firms such as Bibby or Harrison. Its main features were two new docks, long and narrow, connecting with the Herculaneum Entrance to the south and Brunswick Dock to the north. Partly because of a clause inserted in the Act to placate the Birkenhead lobby, Lyster was not allowed to spend his enabled £4,100,000 for the whole project at the rate of more than £500,000 per year, which forced him to tackle the north and south as if they were virtually separate jobs, with the north 'leading'.[63] Although construction at the south end had nominally begun in 1874, it was kept relatively short of funds and by 1881, when Alexandra was opened, expenditure at the sites of the new Harrington and Toxteth docks totalled only £418,129. They eventually opened in 1883 and 1888 respectively, and proved quite successful, producing efficiency figures of £68.8per yard

and £75.3 respectively, and tonnages of 390.3 and 399.3 per yard.[64] Furthermore, they continued to be heavily used well beyond the end-date of this paper. We seem to be set for agreeing with those who made the case for the 'bread and butter ships'. So we would be, had the New North Works been as relatively expensive as the reader might assume from the paragraphs above.

But the South Works had a dark secret. Instead of the works for the exceptional vessels having a higher cost/acre than those for average ones, they had a significantly lower one: the cost per water acre of the North Works was a little high, at just over £30,000, but that of the South Works was nearly £50,000.[65] Some of the reasons are easy to find: the state-of-the-art double-storey transit sheds with their travelling roof cranes at the export berths doubled the achievable throughput per yard of quay, but cost more than twice as much per square foot of floor to build.[66] There was running re-designing going on during the project, involving such things as digging up the sills of the two new docks and re-laying them deeper.[67] But there are other aspects which are less easily explained: the average cost of entrance and passage gates at the North Works was 46s 6d per ft² whereas at the South it was only 32s 10d.[68] Not only is there no obvious reason for this large discrepancy, it also means there must have been much larger ones working in the opposite direction, only one of which is readily discovered. A higher proportion of the new water area had to be excavated from dry land than was the case with the North works, resulting in a much greater volume of spoil per unit area. Furthermore, a great deal of the excavation was in rock which was '…so dead and tough as only to be excavated by blasting. This was a tedious and costly operation…'[69] and, furthermore it produced a large excess of spoil over that required for the backfilling of the new quays, forcing Lyster to buy five hopper barges to take it out to sea and dump it.[70] The result was that excavation at Alexandra cost 2s $2\frac{1}{4}$d per cubic yard while at Toxteth it cost 3s

$1^1/_4$d and the cost at Harrington (2s $11^1/_2$d) was approaching double that at Hornby (1s $7^1/_2$d).[71]

As at the North End, when the new docks opened they were immediately busy, but some at least of their traffic had come from other docks nearby: Brunswick's tonnage and revenue both fell by a third when they opened. Of course, when the modernisation of Brunswick was completed in 1908, its traffic rose by about 50% as compared with its previous average performance—and Toxteth and Harrington showed a slight fall, albeit at a time when the total tonnage through the port was also slightly down. As in the case of the North Works, there is no significant discontinuity in the overall level of business in the port which we could attribute to the completion of the South Works.

This programme also involved a certain amount of rationalisation of the 'system'. As built between 1715 and 1832, the earlier south docks had all been given separate river entrances and enjoyed little or no internal communication with each other. Jesse Hartley had recognised that this was wasteful not only of gatemen's labour but also of total docking capacity, which was effectively governed by the handling capacity of the entrances at high water. Vessels moving from one dock to another ought not to be using the river entrances to do it, thereby getting in the way of vessels arriving or departing, and by the time of his death all the south docks from Georges to Brunswick were connected after a fashion. In the South Works Lyster took a further step along this route, which was completed by his son, of aiming to allow all internal movements to take place within connecting fully-impounded docks. In short, there was expenditure there which was geared to broader system improvement with which it might be unfair to burden the returns from just Toxteth and Harrington. This suggestion seems to be invalidated by evidence already presented: the first and probably largest beneficiary should have been Brunswick, and as we have seen, its earnings fell.

This might be expected to result from vessels cramming into Brunswick during the construction work, which would naturally result in a fall when the work was finished and they could spread themselves again, but comparison of the figures for 1878 (before the works started) and 1890 (after they were completed) shows Brunswick's trade down by almost exactly one third in both revenue and tonnage. However, if we aggregate the tonnage for the whole south dock system from Canning to Herculaneum, we find a very different picture: a rise from 1,022,939 tons of shipping to 1,528,259. Because of the reductions in rates of dues made during the 1880s no direct comparison is possible in money terms, but the percentage tonnage increase is roughly double that for the port as a whole over the same period, and some of that growth must be credited to the 'system improvements' rather than simply to the two main new docks. We may find here some vindication of the policy of building for average-sized ships—for, costly as the South Works were, they cost less than twice as much per acre as those at the north and produced more than twice as much growth.

We would be wrong, because we are not comparing like with like. If the tonnages at the north are aggregated with those of other northern docks we might expect to see suffer as Brunswick did in the south, then over a similar period of twelve years (in this case 1874-1885 to take account of their earlier construction) the comparable group of docks (ie from the northern extremity south to Wellington) shows a rise from 1,937,543 to 3,332,393, a rather higher rate of growth than in the south and achieved at less cost per acre.

But there remains a crucial difference in favour of the south works. Twenty years after construction began—just the sort of time when obsolescence would typically be threatening the need for further major works, Alexandra and Hornby were well on the slide, while Toxteth and Harrington continued to prosper, and when the next great improvement scheme, that under the 1898 Act, came along, they required no significant modernisation. They may not have been a wonderful investment, but they were better than their more ambitious counterparts in the north.

The 1891 Programme

During the 1880s ship sizes continued to rise, and more specifically, their draft increased in relation to their length and beam. The handling capacity of the 'new' north docks became limited not so much by their size or the speed with which vessels could be turned round but by the number of tides in the year and the number of hours on each tide that there was sufficient depth at the Canada entrance for the deeper vessels to come and go. While this problem was the source of numerous complaints and much adverse criticism, it is perhaps in the evidence given in favour of the three Manchester Ship Canal Bills that the issue of 'depth equals time equals money' is most clearly shown.[72] The Board began to attempt to breach the Mersey Bar and laid its plans for the new Sandon Entrances with the fairly clear intention of damaging the prospects of the Ship Canal when it opened. But there was no need to compete with the Ship Canal for the passenger liner traffic: such vessels were already too large to use the canal. The two objectives shared a common solution: a monster half-tide entrance would both accomodate the extra-large ships and extend the time during which medium-to-large vessels could use it, and deepening parts of the 1873 north works would extend similar benefits to a larger water area. The 1891 Dock Act enabled the borrowing of £1,600,000 to carry out deepening of Canada and Huskisson Docks, the construction of a branch to Canada and the disappearance of Sandon (tidal) basin and Wellington half-tide dock under a new deep Sandon half-tide with a very large new entrance.

This is a project of a quite different character in that only the Canada Branch, of a modest $7\frac{1}{2}$ acres, extended rather than improved the accommodation, unless one counts Sandon half-tide as a net gain of just under 11 acres after it took in the former tidal basin. The total water area affected was just under 80 acres, of which slightly over three quarters was re-working of outdated facilities. The opportunity therefore arises to compare two different approaches to the same problem.

In some ways the auguries were better for this scheme than for its predecessor. In 1890 a Special Committee had reported on the Board's system of management and identified many sources of waste and inefficiency, some of which it had eliminated.[73] T. D. Hornby, the elderly and long-standing Chairman had died, arguably opening the way to younger and more adventurous men and G. F. Lyster had gone (or possibly been pushed) into semi-retirement. The affordability of the Board's debt (expressed as the percentage of dues income spent on interest) had been improving, and in 1892 nearly all bond redemptions were of 4-4.5% stock while new issue was at rates between 3.125% and 3.875%. The interest cost of £1,600,000 would therefore be roughly £56,000—and the total revenue in 1902 (the first full year's working after the new entrances opened), exceeded that for 1892 by almost £75,000. That, however is another of the unreasonable comparisons which may tempt us into error: further significant cuts in the rates of dues were made in 1895 and 1896, so that a comparatively modest increase in revenue masks a hefty tonnage increase, from 9,968,697 to 13,308,305. That, perhaps, might be regarded as a sufficiently large growth as to suggest that the new development was a success, but it has to be conceded that the growth was fairly slow and steady and does not show any marked discontinuity as the new facilities came on stream.

If we make more localised comparisons, the result is much the same. Over the same decade, Huskisson rose from 409,912 tons to 940,152, and Canada from 160,092 to a healthy 1,083,566 tons, but Langton and Alexandra fell. However, if as above, we aggregate the figures for the docks from Wellington northwards, a happier picture is revealed, with an increase from 3,662,192 to 5,282,532 tons, or 44% as against 34% for the docks as a whole. Nevertheless, if we compare the rise in

Huskisson's tonnage with the graph showing that tonnage as a percentage of the total for the port, it will be clear that the two curves are very similar: Huskisson's meteoric tonnage rise when the improvements were completed was largely at the expense of other docks within the system.

So great were the technical difficulties of deepening Canada Entrance and underpinning the walls of Canada, Huskisson and Sandon for deepening that the cost per water acre was £20,000, or two thirds of the cost of the North Works under the 1873 Act.[74] The site had more gates and passages to re-build and deepen than there would have been in an all-new design. The triple half-tide entrance, which could also be used as a fully-locked entrance for smaller vessels, was ingenious and successful, but complex and expensive. The works included two large steam-pumped impounding stations at Sandon and Huskisson

which improved the depth of water right through from Hornby to Bramley-Moore, so that the benefits of the investment under the 1891 Act extended well beyond the apparent boundaries of the site.[75] It also included the state-of-the-art three-storey ferro concrete transit sheds at Sandon, and the works were slowed down by the need to keep as much of the system open for as long possible, reducing the efficiency of the works. Viewing the project as a whole, its expense was perhaps rather high but certainly not outrageous.

There was also a strong element of luck. It was built in part to provide an entrance and berths deep enough for the next generation of Atlantic passenger liners, and the guess made as to how big they would be proved a good one this time. When White Star's *Cedric* and sisters came along as the largest ships in the world they could be handled with some ease and when they were supplanted by *Lusitania*

The new Sandon Half-Tide Entrance with one of the White Star Line's 'big four' liners entering. Their move from Alexandra to Huskisson was one of the reasons why Huskisson's revenue rose sharply after the reconstruction programme.

and *Mauretania* those, too, could be accommodated. It was a much better guess than any made for the 1873 programme, and as a result the work was much more successful. In 1921, Huskisson was still the top dock in both tonnage and revenue terms, in each case by a margin approaching 50%. It had been a programme which met the need of its time: it put Liverpool back in the lead, at least temporarily, in the passenger trade and when, over twenty years after it was designed, the biggest liners outgrew the accommodation again, it provided excellent facilities for the 'next size down' which continued to use it heavily.

The interim conclusion, therefore, is that although a global scheme on a muddy mockery of a greenfield site may seem to show compelling advantages in avoidance of technical problems, high unit costs and disruption to existing trade, it was not necessarily like that in real life. The benefits of a more sophisticated engineering approach could outweigh them all.

The Cheap Botch-up

Queens Dock was opened in 1796 and had an area of just over 6.5 acres, extended in 1816 by a little over four acres, which made it briefly the largest dock in the port. The fact that it was in a convenient location meant that its trade held up fairly well during its obsolescence (in 1844 it still ranked fifth in the port in both tonnage and value) but there was no concealing that when it passed into the age of steam it suffered from a number of problems. The first was depth of water—its sill and bottom were only six feet below Old Dock Sill, giving only about 16ft on HWNT[76] and the second was narrow quay margins. Taken together, these meant that by the 1880s its tonnage per yard of quay, at a bit over 120 tons, was poor by the standards of new docks, but good enough to suggest that its popular location would justify a modest investment. In particular, customers always resisted entering a dock in which they might get 'neaped' so that for roughly half of every month the dock's

customers would be small, reluctant or absent. An improved depth of water could be expected to yield a significant increase in traffic.

The problem was not peculiar to Queens: all of the south docks saving only Toxteth, Harrington and Herculaneum, were old and shallow and at least two of them—Kings and Brunswick—shared the same obvious potential for improvement that Queens showed.

The scheme chosen for dealing primarily with Queens, but with benefit to the rest of the system, falls naturally into those components peculiar to Queens and those not. The latter involved some improvements to passage gates to enable them to control a greater head of water and fitting them with hydraulic motors to increase their speed of operation, but the principal component was the construction of the Coburg impounding station, with its associated culverts, to raise water from the river into the dock system. Three huge steam pumps delivered up to 1,200 tons of water per minute, allowing the level to be kept at around HWST, giving a depth of about 24ft in Queens Dock.[77]

The main problem peculiar to Queens was the constricted nature of the landward side of its site, where a small street came right to the back of the transit sheds, which themselves were nowhere near wide enough for discharging steamers of the class which the Board hoped would soon be wooed to the dock by the deeper water. To provide a new and larger shed required the acquisition of some land, and the decision was taken to secure the land as far up as the next street inland—the present-day Dock Road. This was done, so far as possible, piecemeal and in secret to avoid the inevitable price rise which would occur once it became known that the Board was buying. However, the Board at this time held Parliamentary powers to build the future Liverpool Overhead Railway—and to compulsorily purchase such of the land required as they did not already own.[78] They promptly gained authority for a 'deviation' to the route which sent it straight through the property of those hanging on for an extortionate price. None the less, the fairly small amount of land involved cost a total of £47,313 on leasehold and a further £6,040 on freehold at prices up to £8 per square yard.[79] These payments were made from the Board's Land Account, one of a number of 'stashes' which the Board used for carrying short-term surplus revenue through from year to year.

So far, this sounds like an appropriate little scheme for providing extra capacity at low cost, undertaken in the knowledge both that it might only last about ten years and that it would be a useful stopgap. It had the further advantage that because it could be paid for out of revenue and needed no new compulsory purchase powers there was no need to incur the expense and delay of going to Parliament. Once it was complete it well more than doubled Queens Dock's typical annual dues income from around £11,000 before to around £29,000 afterwards.

The problem is that it was not, in fact, all that cheap a scheme. The *Engineer's Report and Accounts* for 1888, when work started in earnest, show a total project expenditure for the year of £22,204, which was followed by £16,102 in 1889 and £10,586 in 1890.[80] That saw the pump house built and commissioned, all the levelling culverts completed and hydraulic motors fitted to the passage gates, and a negligible expenditure in 1891 tempts us to think it it was all over. But there was a shed mentioned above, which was built and paid for in 1892, at a cost of £41,253 and the small matter of paying the Corporation £10,000 for the widening and 'reconstruction' of the Dock Road. The 'low-budget' project has already cost a minimum of £154,000—a little over the yardstick cost for a new dock the size of Queens.[81] The Board's new borrowing at this time was mostly at $3\,^{3}/_{4}\%$, so we should expect a marginal revenue of at least £5,775 to reach a notional break-even point. That, however, is not enough, for large pumping stations needed large amounts of coal and men to shovel it, shift engineers to supervise the machinery and so on. The running costs of Coburg pumping

station in 1892 (its first full year's work) were £3,461, and this figure does not include the marginal costs of extra dredging necessitated by the operation of the pumps.[82] There is almost certainly some further expenditure 'hidden' in some unlikely place in the accounts, for the men in Lyster's office were very good at that, and in the real world outside the Dock Board it would be necessary to make allowance for depreciation, which the Board never did except on its floating plant.[83] Even so, it looks a good-value scheme.

As one might expect, the revenue from the coastwise trade at Queens fell, and that from trades using larger vessels (including the USA trade) rose. But it is an unfortunate fact that, once again, although the total tonnage and revenue at Queens both rose handsomely, those at adjoining docks fell. If we aggregate the figures for all the docks served by the new impounding pumps for the years 1887 (before work started) and 1893 (the first full year after it was completed) we find a rise only from £75,366 to £80,546. Now it must be admitted that 1893 was not a good trading year and the total revenue of the Board grew only by about 8% over the same period, but 1895 was a good year. Both the port's total tonnage and total revenue reached new record levels, hidden within which was a further small rise at Queens, and a much larger one to £87,540 in the Brunswick-Wapping aggregate.

Exactly what was happening is unclear, though one might suspect that, since all these ageing docks benefited equally from the deeper water and the power-operated gates, it was the raised quayside and the new shed which simply moved Queens up the local pecking order. Almost equally unclear is the situation at Albert, where tonnage trebled between 1889 and 1894. Some members of the Board attributed the rise to the impounding pumps, but they did so before they saw an almost equally precipitate fall in 1898-99, and in their unpunctured optimism there was even talk of enlarging the passages at Albert to accommodate wider as well as deeper vessels. Milne and Tonks[84] take the rather more pragmatic view that this was another case of Engineer-dodging, and certainly the timing of the rise and fall coincide pretty closely with the closure and re-opening of Canada Lock, work which caused intense difficulty at the north end.

What is clear, however, is that in the short term the scheme represented better value for money than did the larger-scale ones considered above.

In the longer term, the need for the impounding system was greatly reduced by the huge reconstruction works under the 1898 Dock Act, which included dredging Queens to 19ft 6in below Old Dock Sill. In 1908, the very year that programme was completed, one of the Coburg pumps was moved to the Huskisson Impounding Station to increase its capacity and the remaining two were laid up. Those works also altered Queens almost beyond recognition, with the construction of two branch docks and a new large graving dock between the old part of the dock and the river, but the east wall remained in place, as did the 'new' shed, which was cleaned and painted in 1902 and survived until the May blitz of 1941.

Conclusions

In the cases studied, adaptations financially out-performed new-build despite their sometimes greater unit cost and other apparent disadvantages. Furthermore, percentage returns seem to be more or less inversely related to the size and cost of the scheme, though it must be emphasised that by the standards of most industries at the time none of the schemes was particularly small. It might be thought that this is because large schemes were built ahead of growth in trade, providing space for future needs and only producing a fair return in the longer term, but this does not appear to be invariably so: the New North Works 'peaked' very quickly and showed the first signs of obsolescence much sooner than the approximate '20-year rule' derived from narrative sources would suggest they should have done.[85] This offers the obvious temptation to conclude that qualitative engineering issues are more important than those of trade or finance, but the New South Works were built by essentially the same team as the North Works, and Toxteth and Harrington proved singularly successful in maintaining their trade. Of the engineering issues which might be thought to divide the north and south works under the 1873 Act, the obvious one is that there was significantly more innovation involved in the north, including a hugely complex silt-sluicing system, new dry-dock pumping technology and a monster 100-ton hydraulic crane at Langton. Neither the sluicing nor the crane was wholly successful, but what scuppered this group of docks was, beyond reasonable doubt, their insufficient depth of water. The sills at Toxteth and Harrington—intended for smaller vessels— were actually deeper.

This is where size becomes a major factor. Constructing a new and deeper half-tide entrance as in the 1891 works may be complex and expensive, but it is an up-date of a bona-fide obsolete facility: deepening a fairly new 44-acre dock is another matter. The cost of rectifying any mistake relates to the size of the job in which it occurred. But size also affects the attempt to keep up with obsolescence. If a project is, as it should be, geared to cope with future growth rather than simply to cure present congestion, then the bigger its quayage, the longer it will take to reach full capacity and the more generous its specification will have to be if it is not to become obsolete before it breaks even. It is a self-exciting feedback loop of size and cost in which only the boldest and the richest can succeed.[86] Avoiding that loop is what, at opposite ends of the price scale, the Canada-Huskisson improvements and the Queens Dock scheme achieved, the 1873 south works partly achieved and the 1873 north works emphatically did not.

The Board members often discussed the question of how far ahead they should try and plan. What seems to emerge from the case studies above is that the more ambitious the development, the further ahead it was necessary to be able to see in their crystal ball and the heavier the penalties for getting it wrong. Conversely, with a cheap short-term programme, there was more chance of correctly predicting its performance and much less waste if it failed. In short, while the traditional view that it was necessary to be bold and far-sighted in planning dock improvements is borne out by events in some cases, it is by no means a universal truth. In dock design as in life, 'I am bold and far-sighted, you are over-confident, he is foolhardy'.

The Effective Size of Port Facilities: A Liverpool Case Study.[87]

It is usual for the historians of fully-docked ports to do as their predecessors, the port engineers and managers, used to do and assess the capacity of the port in terms of a water area and a total lineal quayage, with gradual increases as the port grows to suit a growing trade. With the passage of time, the area of land becomes proportionately more important as railway tracks and their space-gobbling curves are installed. As ships get larger in cross-section and hence in cargo density,[88] so too must the sheds that serve them, and the areas behind the sheds must get wider.

Except when a dock or group of docks was both large and new, it only took a modest up-turn in trade to start the customers complaining about goods being delayed by congestion on the quayside, and these complaints usually led rapidly to a demand for new docks. If the complainants were successful, this led to a Bill being laid before Parliament and most such Bills were contested, resulting in a Select Committee enquiry.[89] The minutes of evidence of these enquiries form a wonderful 'snapshot source' for the history of the port at that particular time. Typically the first witness for the Bill will produce figures showing a steady growth of traffic through the port and explain the benefit to the shipping industry at large, and hence to the nation's trade, of the proposed new development. Such witnesses have often emerged in older historical studies as 'men of vision'. Their engineers, while not beatified in the Samuel Smiles manner and hence much less known than Smiles' subjects, are none the less portrayed as quasi-heroic figures without whose skills the vision could not be implemented. Conversely, objectors, while not demonised in the manner of some of the objectors to early railway construction,[90] tend to emerge as men incapable of taking a long

view, a judgement which is almost invariably 'confirmed' by subsequent growth in trade.

Such a view definitely needs re-examination. Jackson has questioned the need to build the Birkenhead Docks at all, and the present author has pointed out that the dire prophecies of the opponents of the Manchester Ship Canal were in fact all fulfilled and the Port of Manchester survived only through heavy subsidy from the Manchester City Council[91] and on the fruits of property developments which formed no part of the scheme as put before Parliament. The reasons for the adoption of the interpretation which this paper sets out to challenge are not hard to find: not only do some of the sources contain an in-built bias towards 'progress', but in several cases the first or leading published history of a particular port was written by an 'insider' who set out to establish just such a picture of 'men of vision'.[92] But did British ports, and Liverpool in particular, have to expend quite so many millions of capital in the period 1870-1914?

In fact, it is by no means certain that extension of dock facilities is the best or only way of increasing the capacity of a port, and while that statement applies chiefly if one judges capacity by the throughput of goods, it is partially defensible even when the yardstick is the maximum size of ship which the system can handle.

The maximum size of ship able to use a particular berth or dock entrance is not determined only by what it says on the original engineer's drawings for the construction: there are maintenance and minor alteration factors to be taken into consideration as well, of which by far the most important is dredging. Liverpool Docks suffered badly from silting, and the greater the depth of water which existed on the engineer's drawing, the greater its diminution in real life by silt. Similarly, in the days of hydraulic lime mortars, apparently inelastic masonry could move without suffering failure: an invert in a passage could rise or a wall in a lock bulge, resulting again in a small discrepancy between the drawing and what the harbourmaster's men knew were the real dimensions.

These, however, are minor considerations. Far more important is the issue of whether a dock system should be continuously modernised to keep abreast of new needs rather than being enlarged on a cyclical basis of under-provision, construction, over-provision. This apppproach to dock engineering is not invalidated by the constant growth of trade in the period with which this paper is primarily concerned, for a successful re-working of an old dock or docks could easily bring about such a rise in tonnage per yard of quay as to meet the needs of growing trade for several years. What does render it highly suspect is the slow and technically difficult nature of such work, which can result in a cost per water acre as great as that of new construction.[93] A second serious disadvantage is the amount of time that the working area of the dock estate as a whole is diminished by the engineer and his men taking possession of part of it, normally for years at a time and in the (fortunately unusual) case of the Canada-Huskisson improvements, for nearly ten years. The serious inconvenience such works caused to the port's customers may be seen from the way in which they moved round the estate to avoid the men with the shovels. Even Albert Dock, when in the latter stages of obsolescence, had a marked upturn in trade between 1891 and 1900, coinciding more or less with the works at Canada-Huskisson.[94]

In works of such scale, the Engineer could do no right, for the remedy for each problem exacerbated the other. One of the tasks was underpinning the old walls of Huskisson to enable the deepening of the dock. The simple and obvious way to do this was to drain the dock—but that would have completely incapacitated some two miles of quay for a considerable time. The alternative was to do the work 'piecemeal' behind curved temporary dams. But these had first to be constructed in a graving dock and then stored somewhere for re-use. One of those used was 260ft long, 30ft wide and 39ft high, requiring a lot of 'somewhere' to put it.[95] Some of these structures were stored for long periods:

There are still in use on the Liverpool Dock Estate flitches [temporary dams] which the author constructed years ago, and which will, in all probability, be used when the present generation has long been forgotten.[96]

Similarly, trade through much of the southern system was heavily disrupted by the major reconstruction works under the 1898 Dock Act at Kings, Queens, Coburg and Brunswick Docks, a total of over 40 acres of water. The quality of the finished job was good both in design and execution, but with completion taking until 1908, the price was again almost a decade of disruption. But when modernisations reached this scale they were conceptually little different from new build projects. In the previous paper I have suggested that the likelihood of an improvement scheme being financially viable was in almost inverse proportion to its size and ambition. The further ahead the 'men of vision' had to look, the less likely they were to get it right. One thing this paper seeks to tease out is, first, whether it was possible to make significant improvements in the throughput of a given facility by still cheaper or simpler means, and, if so, whether that approach is a construct of hindsight or the Mersey Docks & Harbour Board knew of it at the time.

There are some cases where both questions may be simply and easily answered in the affirmative. An example was the purchase of the tug *Hodgson* (1883), whose purpose was to tow out small sailing vessels from Canada Entrance as early as possible on the rising tide, free of charge, thus allowing more of the time available before the ebb set in for the large steamships.[97] It was a simple and modest investment which may be seen as a straight alternative to increasing the capacity of the entrance by ripping up thousands of tons of masonry to enlarge it. Furthermore, it was clearly successful and its success was recognised by the Board, for when the New South Works under the 1873 Act were finally completed in 1888, the *Neptune* was purchased to do the same job there. At an earlier date, the capacity of entrances had been enlarged by an arguably even simpler method: the application of hydraulic power to the gates of Canada Entrance significantly reduced the time spent in opening and closing the gates by hand, which increased the availability of the entrance by almost 50%.[98] By contrast, further increasing its capacity, by deepening and lengthening the lock, involved its closure from 1890-95, causing severe inconvenience to the users of Hornby, Alexandra, Langton and Brocklebank docks while some 41,000 cubic yards of masonry and concrete were laid.[99]

The non-trading use of water space

The advertised, as distinct from the effective, water area of the docks is customarily inflated in a number of ways. For example, the total water area and lineal quayage quoted in the Board's *Yearbook* for 1920 includes Brunswick Half-tide. Now this was only a tiny dock, making up less than 1% of the water area of the Liverpool system, but the fact is that it was not available for trading vessels, because it was used as a repair dock by the engineer's department, and what he was repairing was a considerable fleet of the Board's own vessels— in his department alone there were five sandpump dredgers, six ladder dredgers, seven grab dredgers,[100] fifteen steam hopper barges, five floating cranes including the 200-ton lift *Mammoth* and 11 'flats'. When we add in the rest of the Board's fleet, we have a substantial dock-full of shipping, larger than the fleets of many of the port's paying customers. Now many of these vessels could be, and were, berthed in obsolescent or obsolete docks like Albert or Stanley, but the fact remains that they represent a permanent deduction from the nominal capacity of the system. In the case of the sandpump dredgers,

although they were quite often out dredging at the bar or in the outer approach channels, when they did need berthing, they required good quality berths for their aggregate length of well over 1,500 ft.[101]

The mention of seven grab dredgers should also sound an alarm bell: these craft were for use purely within the dock system, which means that at any one time perhaps four berths[102] would be unavailable because of dredging—which also involved one or more of the steam hopper barges (some of which were as much as 1,200 nrt) being there as well, to take the dredgings out to sea. These hopper barges also made extensive demands on the ship-handling capacity of the entrances: in the late 1880s they were passing in and out of dock some 6,000+ times per year carrying, *inter alia*, some 600,000 tons of dredgings

There is another entire category of annoyances for customers which needs to be taken into account. We have touched upon the activities of the engineer's department in major construction mode, but there was also a continuum of maintenance works and minor improvements being carried out on revenue account.

Because of the scale of operation of the port and the age of some of its structures, these 'minor' works could in fact be large enough to put several more berths out of commission at any one time. Clarence Half-tide, for example, one of the busiest parts of the entire dock estate, was run dry 14-18 November 1898 for overhauling the gates, and it and the Trafalgar Lock were run dry in January 1899.[103] At the same time, the Victoria-Trafalgar passage was undergoing heavy improvement works and the west quay of Trafalgar had its shed demolished and a new one built, putting the quay out of commission for months. Princes Half-tide was run dry for a week in August 1898,[104] and Canning and Canning Half-tide were run dry on 25 January 1898. These works, which mainly affected the coasting trade, were going on at the same time as major capital works at both north and south ends.

Nor was the engineer done yet. Works of

any size, whatever their nature, required extra space for storage of materials, and construction not just of sections of timber dams but other large temporary works as well.[105] Normally this space could be found in sheds or on quaysides which were already rendered inoperable by the main works, but this was not invariably the case and sometimes addtional land was needed. This is an issue which was rarely mentioned in reports or minutes, but even a perfunctory examination of photographs of construction works[106] will reveal the scale on which operations proceeded, involving the handling and storage of huge quantities of timber, stone, mortar etc. inwards and of hundreds of thousand of cubic yards of spoil outwards. Adding to the congestion of the roads and railways of the dock estate was the oft-forgotten supply of coal for the working plant, which was not negligible: the Canada-Huskisson scheme consumed some 26,000 tons between 1892 and 1897.[107] A temporary dam could only begin to qualify as 'large' if it contained more than 1,000 tons of timber.

Maintenance work on movable bridges was mainly an annoyance to road users rather than a factor in temporarily disabling berths, though obstruction of either of the passages at Coburg Dock would cut Kings and Queens docks off from the river for any vessel which could not use the little Canning Half-tide entrance. But many of the bridges of the estate were old and others were badly designed, with the result that at any one time there was about a 50% chance that a bridge would be out of service somewhere on the estate.[108]

Clutter

There is, however, another factor diminishing the actual capability of the dock system which has passed unnoticed by historians and which might loosely be termed 'clutter'. In an age where shipowners and consignees could have bitter disputes between themselves or in triangular contests with the Board over quite trifling amounts of goods it seems unthinkable that there should be goods left in the Board's

warehouses for years on end without their being claimed, and in many cases without the Board being able to trace their current owner.[109] Not only did this happen, it happened so frequently that the Warehouse Committee considered the sale of unclaimed goods of one sort or another at roughly one third of all its meetings. The reasons for the goods being abandoned vary, including clerical error and the death of a sole consignee, but by far the largest cause was that goods had been left in the warehouses for so long that the charges on them exceeded their value. For this reason, we find that a high proportion of the abandoned goods is made up of goods bearing a high rate of duty, such as the 12 cases of brandy the Committee resolved should be sold on 1 February 1893. The brandy was, of course, in bond, so to sell it the Board had to pay the duty on it and in that instance, as in the majority of sales, the Board had to write off a small loss on the transaction. While most of the unclaimed consignments were small, we find 28 casks of soda ash here, 105 cases of cheese there.

Despite the fact that income from 'Rummage Sales' appears in the Board's published accounts, the Warehouse Committee's policy in the late 1870s was to consider at least some consignments individually, in part because they were afraid of exceeding their powers under the Mersey Docks & Harbour Board (Consolidation) Act of 1858. Their success in disposing of goods without any serious legal embarrassment, coupled with the fact that the problem was obviously growing, caused the Board to delegate to the Secretary power to hold the 'rummage sales' at the warehouses as and when he thought it necessary.[110] It was necessary about once a month, but there is no clear trend in the accounts during the years for which the proceeds of the sales were included, so whether or not this policy helped free up warehouse space cannot be told with any certainty.

The same principle applied to ships. In 1877, the Board sold a schooner called *Sarah Jane* for the modest sum of £10. She had been lying in the West Float, Birkenhead for about four years, her owner could not be traced and the Marine Surveyor considered her to be in a dangerous condition. Unsurprisingly, the unpaid dues on her amounted to more than £10. Three other 'wrecks' were sold from other berths in the same year, and in the case of the schooner *Satellite* the buyer, probably wisely, had second thoughts so the Board sold her again.[111] Although all the vessels were small, it is clear that at any one time the nominal lineal quayage of the port was reduced by several hundred feet occupied by 'wrecks'.

From the same source, we learn of another source of lost capacity, namely vessels which sank in dock. The causes were various and included collision and capsize through incompetent loading or discharge, but the majority were 'flats' which simply foundered through old age and lack of maintenance. In 1899, for example, 18 'flats' sank in dock and while some were raised immediately because they were in particularly obstructive positions, others lay for days.[112] Among the 18 were, shame to admit it, two of the Engineer's 'flats', whose sinkings were reported to the Docks & Quays Committee on 31 May and 6 August respectively. The Engineer's men raised them themselves, thus avoiding the humiliation of an internal recharge from the Water Bailliff.

The Board, like many organisations of its day, was passionate about avoiding what it perceived as waste. Some of the unclaimed goods in the warehouses were consignments of

A busy scene at Huskisson No. 1 Branch, with a state-of-the-art three storey transit shed. But look carefully at the mid-ground extreme left of the picture: there is a heap of clutter there at least the length of four horses and their wagons and the width of two.

tobacco, and while undamaged cases of good cigars were worth selling, damaged or low-quality tobacco or tobacco products were unlikely to realise as much as the duty payable on them, so they were 'destroyed'—incinerated—under the supervision of HM Customs. On 14 May 1884 the Warehouse Committee received an offer of 2s 6d per ton for tobacco ash, which was apparently useful to fertiliser manufacturers. When we read of people complaining about congestion on the quays of the port, we have to remember that a few square yards somewhere were occupied by tobacco ash, (which is not very dense) being piled up until there was enough to make it worth selling. Of course, a few square yards was not significant, or so it seems until we look at the number of other things being re-cycled in this way.

Sweepings were big business. Wherever tea or tobacco was handled, the floor sweepings were kept (in bond, of course) until, once again, there were several tons and then they were offered for sale. A prolonged dispute broke out in the summer and autumn of 1885 over the ownership of 24 tons of guano sweepings at Birkenhead Warehouses. Quay sweepings, which contained a high proportion of horse manure, were, naturally, gathered up and stored until there was a canal boatful—about 40 tons—to despatch to farms along the Leeds and Liverpool Canal.[113] The storing-up was done at one of three waste depots provided by the Engineer, each occupying a berth about 120ft long. The most prolific producers of sweepings, though, were the corn warehouses at Waterloo Dock and at Birkenhead: in the early years of last century they were producing around 12 tons of 'machinery floor sweepings' per month, sold to animal feed millers for, typically, around 35s 0d per ton. More wasted storage space.

But at least it brought in a small revenue. At Albert and Stanley warehouses we find they had some scrap wood—described as 'a quantity of wood chips', and the Warehouse Committee generously decided to offer these *gratis* to local charitable institutions for firewood, provided the institutions collected them for themselves. On 21 November 1900 the Warehouse Committee received a report that the institutions had taken all they wanted, amounting to some 40 [cart] loads, but that another 50 loads remained. A typical Liverpool cart of the period would certainly carry more than a cubic yard of 'wood chips', so at least 100 cubic yards of prime and profitable[114] warehouse space had been filled with material which the Board could not even give away.

The following year, the Warehouse Committee continued to have a clear-out: at their meeting of 18 December 1901 they authorised the sale of, *inter alia*, five tons of 'old iron shutters' and three tons of 'scrap iron' at Stanley warehouses, 12-15 cwt of old 'River Plate Bands' [from bales of wool] and 4cwt of 'scraps' [of bale bands] from the wool warehouse.[115] From the Esparto Shed, Birkenhead, went two tons of old iron hoops and the Birkenhead Warehouse had five tons of old chain. The real gem of uselessness, though, was from Albert: 4 tons of 'short pieces of old iron bands'.

But the real bulk of rubbish was always going to be generated by the Engineer's Department. As early as 1827 the published accounts of the Trustees of the Liverpool Docks show receipt of £616 for the sale of old iron and ropes, with another £929 for old building materials. In the much more complex situation which obtained late in the century it was only to be expected that there would be more rubbish. What is less clear why it was allowed to accumulate in large quantities before steps were taken to sell it. In 1877, for example, 9 tons of old rope, 9 tons of spelter dross, 160 tons of wrought iron scrap, 120 tons of old sheet iron and 250 tons of old rail were sold from the Dock Yard, along with significant amounts from other locations, including another 950 tons of old rails.[116] Sales by tender of large amounts of scrap metal and other old materials became an annual event, and when we find that the 1893 sale included 250 tons mixed iron and steel scrap, 50 tons of old chain, 10 tons of old rope and 20 tons of broken glass we seem to be looking at just one year's production of rubbish.

In fact, there was even more rubbish than that, for several of the successful tenderers in 1893 observed additional quantities of scrap when they went to collect their purchases and wrote to the Board asking if they might purchase that as well—including another 100 tons of mixed scrap at the Dock yard. In the 1894 sale there are 63$\frac{1}{2}$ pairs of 'old scuttlers long boots'. Scuttling was the old-fashioned method of getting silt out of a dock: a number of mud 'flats' were placed in it and the gates shored open so that the dock dried out at low water. The scuttlers, in their long boots, shovelled mud into the flats until either they were full or the water came back. It had been practised for many years only for clearing out gate recesses and small corners at passages where the dredgers could not reach. 63$\frac{1}{2}$ pairs was not the end of the story of the boots, for in 1894 another 24 pairs were sold, and then in 1900 another 50 pairs. All the time, hundreds of tons of scrap were being sold. Keeping 85 empty powder kegs until the 1900 sale (they realised 3d each) might not have been the most effective use of space in the Dock Yard, and since the Engineer's men had long since been using Tonite for most blasting purposes, the kegs had probably been there quite some time. Such are the quantities of materials being sold off that one can legitimately query whether, if they were sold off frequently in small lots, it would have been necessary for the Engineer to retain both his Northern Dock Yard and his Central Dock Yard in addition to the original Dock Yard at Coburg—and his three rubbish depots, each occupying a berth suitable for a fair-sized coaster.

A. G. Lyster, Engineer-in-Chief, knew this perfectly well, and at a meeting of the Works Committee on 16 February 1900, he sought and received authority to hold sales four times per year. It was a fine idea, but in the first of these quarterly sales there were, believe it or not, 72 pairs of scuttlers' boots, which someone had presumably retained in case they came in useful. Perhaps more discouraging is that in

the third sale of the new low-junk regime there appeared yet another 50 pairs of boots.

It might be thought that the Engineer's rubbish problems did not impinge on the users of the port except through the need to occupy the three depots, but such is not the case. Because the Dock Yards and depots became over-loaded, rubbish backed up on the quays. In 1898, for example, there were three tons of broken glass at North Huskisson No 2 and another eight tons at East Alexandra No 1. The following year there were 30 tons of scrap timber at East Huskisson No 3 and another 15 at Canada Branch. These were prime berths in a newly-modernised part of the system, even if the new Sandon Entrance was not yet complete to serve them. These, of course, are only examples of the rubbish we know about because it was offered for sale. There was probably a great deal more, and the customers had been doing their bit as well, if we may judge from the edict of the Docks & Quays Committee of 14 March 1883 to the effect that 'ash bins' should not exceed 12ft x 6ft x 4ft deep or exceed 5% of the area of an appropriated berth.

This was always going to be a particular problem for Liverpool, for compared with many British ports it had always endured high land acquisition costs[117] and as a result successive engineers had been a little mean with 'back space', placing a premium on efficient porterage to get goods to and from the water's edge. Clearly it was impossible to work berths without generating rubbish, but equally clearly it was essential to keep every last square foot as clear as humanly possible and this simply was not done. There was a culture of poor housekeeping at every level.

In 1911, the Board appointed a Special Committee which was to investigate the conduct of the Board's business, which it did very thoroughly, making its final report in 1913. Strangely, although it suggested major changes in the Engineer's department, including complete re-location of the Dock Yard and what amounted to dividing the Engineer-in-Chief's post in two and making

'Just put it somewhere out of the way for now!'

both new posts subordinate to the General Manager and Secretary, no direct comments about the level of non-availability of berths appear. The Committee did question whether the rubbish depot at Clarence Half-tide could not be moved to 'a less valuable site', but the Docks & Quays Committee decided 'in the special circumstances… not to interfere'.[118] The expression 'in the special circumstances' is a coded one which often appears in Board and Committee minutes, and its meaning is 'we know this decision appears inconsistent/irrational/wrong-headed, but we are doing it anyway and we are not going to tell you why'. This might be taken to imply that the Special Committee had not found anything much wrong in the area of scrap disposal and general clutter. In fact it had, but the response was, again, coded. One of its recommendations was

that a member of the General Manager's staff, preferably accompanied by a couple of members of the Board, should go round all the Departments once a year 'for the purpose of ascertaining whether there are in such storeyards any articles not required…' The meaning of this was that those principal officers who had 'storeyards', chiefly the Engineer, the Marine Surveyor and the Chief Warehouse Manager', were simply not to be trusted not to store loads of rubbish.

One 'commodity' on which the archives are very thin is ballast. What we do know is that it was at the warehouse docks (which were for imports only) that it was most likely to be wanted and least likely to arrive in the normal course of things, unless as 'stiffening' in a bulky cargo of relatively low weight. Clearly somebody took ballast which had been discharged at sheds or open quays to the warehouses, for there were frequent disputes about ballast at the Waterloo Corn Warehouses, and Recommendation 10 of the Special Committee was that 'the kentledge [iron ballast] which is on hand at the warehouses and which is not now earning any appreciable revenue, be disposed of…' At first, the Warehouse Committee decided to keep it, but then at their meeting of 11 June 1913 decided it could go. Unfortunately no quantity is mentioned, and the published Accounts give only the surplus for each warehouse with no detail of income and expenditure, so it is impossible to estimate how much 'dead space' was created by ballast. There does seem to have been a practice of allowing people to leave quite large quantities of pig iron on the south quay of Canning Half-tide for months at a time and for a very low rental, but whether this was in fact ballast or cargo is unclear. The term 'kentledge' was more usual for ballast at the time.[119]

Similarly, there are infuriating passing mentions of 'the Board's coal tips': I have yet to discover where, in normal conditions, these were or how large they were: coal contracts give no delivery address, which was given only on individual orders, which have not survived. The deliveries were, however, clearly substantial as the annual total of steam coal was over 20,000 tons on the Liverpool side alone in 1888.[120] Following the purchase of the large sandpump dredgers and the construction of further pumping stations, coal consumption, and with it coal stocks, rose rapidly.[121] But on this, even the Special Committee is silent: its only mention of coal is a recommendation that the Board's yacht (they called it a 'tender') *Galatea* could exist on a diet of North Wales coal as used in all the other vessels, instead of South Wales, at an estimated saving of £300 per year.[122]

The Special Committee was working against a background of intense discontent among port users with acute congestion of the quays and avenues of the docks brought about by the considerable revival in trade which

began in 1911. The Chamber of Commerce appointed a Committee for the Improvement of Transport in Liverpool which also produced a report in 1913.[123] This is an interesting document, because it breaks the mould mentioned at the beginning of this paper: it is highly critical of the Board, but it does not repeat the fallacy that what was needed was more docks: it fully recognised that there were enough docks, and even grudgingly admitted that the Board had done well in spending money on more efficient sheds. Instead, we find a realisation that such factors as cargo-handling equipment and 'ships' gear' left lying around can be highly disruptive, and on 10 December 1913, the Dock & Quays Committee heard that the Chief Traffic Manager had already 'taken steps to curtail, as far as possible, the space occupied by ships' gear, propellors, tail shafts etc inside and outside the sheds at appropriated berths.' This, of course, also reflected an aspect of the behaviour of shipowners of which consignees had long complained: they would discharge all night and all day to get their ships away from the import berths, caring not a jot what chaos they might leave on the quayside through the lumpers outpacing the porters and the porters outpacing the carters while obstructing the work of both the latter groups with their own junk, left lying around.

So far as I can estimate,[124] between 1873 and 1908, up to 10% of the port's quays were in the hands of the engineer for major works for nearly all the time. At least another 1% was undergoing minor maintenance of a disruptive kind and about 2% of the water area was occupied by the Board's own vessels, whether moored or at work. We may find as much as another 0.5% occupied by wrecks, vessels under arrest etc. and a further 0.5% was occupied by rubbish. Even if the exact percentages are slightly suspect, these are certainly the main causes of non-availability, and in correct order of incidence.[125] Set against the engineering mayhem, the poor housekeeping seems insignificant. But some quaysides *were* permanently occupied with rubbish, and the worse the inescapable causes of non-availability, such as dredging, got, the more important it was to eliminate the minor ones, for they became a larger proportion of the *potentially available* total.[126] Given the narrow avenues and quay margins on much of the system, it did not require much scrap wood or metal lying around to prevent one cart passing another at a 'pinch'—a pinch which might well have been created by a berth-holder taking up his full allocation of 5% for his ash bins.

The Cost

In short, this is another instance of our needing to investigate how ports really worked, rather than how they were said to. Although some of the space used for storing rubbish was not prime earning ground, it is worth remembering that 0.5% of the Board's dues income in 1910 amounted to over £6,400, a significant sum in the light of the economy measures proposed by the Special Committee. We also need to re-examine our methods of comparing port efficiency, for the during the period considered here, the Port of Liverpool was effectively only about seven eighths the size we thought it was. Have we, in fact, found another and potentially useful, means of comparing port efficiency? Should we be measuring and comparing the percentage of ports' quayage which is *actually in use*?

Ultimately, the consequences in Liverpool were further-reaching than that: this paper began with demands for new docks and it ends with the recognition that some of that demand arose only because of existing dock space being unavailable, some of it through sheer bad housekeeping. A really thorough-going clear-out and clean-up and a ruthless purge on wrecks in about 1900 would have produced the berthing equivalent of a small new dock of about 5 acres, virtually free of charge. It would not be fair to compare the space thus gained with a brand new deep water dock, but marking it down to half price would still represent a capital saving of some £125,000[127] and a bond interest saving at the rates then prevailing of £4,375 pa. Similarly, one could not assume an average dues earning rate per yard of quay, but assuming an only modest efficiency, it would provide berthing for at least 50,000 tons of shipping per year, which at the average 'take' of £0.11/register ton would yield dues of £5,500, placing the total annual cost of clutter in the region of £10,000pa. That may seem small beer in an organisation of such size, but it must be remembered that in 1908 construction of Gladstone Dock had to be halted for lack of funds. The Board's finances at this time were decidedly fragile.

I have remarked before on Gordon Jackson's uncanny ability to produce a correct analysis of facts of which he is not yet aware. He it was who first questioned the need for all of the dock construction which took place in the period considered in this paper. He was concerned chiefly with economic need: I have tried to show that, at least in a small measure, the physical need has been overplayed as well.

The last word

I am most grateful to Peter Lucas, recently retired as Chief Engineer of the Mersey Docks & Harbour Company, for reading the first draft of this paper. I specifically asked him if he thought I was pushing the 'clutter' argument too far. His response was that it was still applicable when he came to Liverpool in 1968, and remembered that as a new member of the department one of the first tasks he had been given was to try and purge the Dock Yard of rubbish. He did not, unfortunately, recall finding any scuttlers' boots, but he did suggest that at some future stage I should research the sex life of the portable quayside shed. These little structures, used as temporary offices or equipment stores, apparently still caused problems in his time by proliferating overnight.

Appendix: A summary of engineering activity in 1895

1895 has been chosen for a 'spot check' because it is a bad, though by no means the worst, year for engineering activities occupying quay space and disrupting trade. It should be pointed out that the Board's Accounting Year was 1 August to 31 July, so these events, extracted from the *Engineer's Report,* relate to 1894-95 rather than the calendar year 1895.

Capital works

From the North:

Major masonrywork and shed construction on North Quay of Hornby Dock. (approx 600 yards of quay)

East Alexandra No. 3: warehouse construction (65 yards)

Canada Entrance lock closed.

Canada: masonrywork on north, west, and south-east walls (c400yards)

Canada-Huskisson passage closed.

Huskisson west wall, north end being re-aligned (c50 yds)

Sandon basin, north-east corner, underpinning of walls (c.100 yds)

One of two Sandon-Huskisson locks closed

Wellington H-T, underpinning (c120 yds)

Wellington H-T entire west side given over to construction of new river entrances (c200 yards)

Stanley, South side of dock being infilled to build new tobacco warehouse (c250 yds)

Princes Dock/H-T Re-alignment of railway, (c60yds)

South of Princes, the only capital works in hand did not involve taking possession of berth space, but the approximate berth loss to capital works was 1845 yards, and this must be taken as a very optimistic figure, because it makes no allowance for extra quayage taken over as working space. It was at the very least equivalent to being permanently without a fairly large and newish dock such as Langton, including its branch. Unencumbered, in the late '80s, Langton typically earned just under £70,000 pa.

Maintenance Works.

This, however, is by no means the end of the losses in unusable space, major maintenance items, of the sort lasting several weeks or more, including installing a public weighbridge at Langton Branch, road repairs at Hornby, Canada, South Carriers, removal of railway lines at Canada and repairs to shed floors at several more docks created circulation problems for vehicles, while works on the river entrances at Princes, Canning and Brunswick T-T meant that only half the river entrances remained open all year. There were extensive shed reconstruction works at Princes, putting some 700 yards of quay out of action for part of the year. Clearly the Engineer felt he may as well be hung for a sheep, since he also closed the Princes river entrance and the passages to East and West Waterloo for brief periods while the railway works were going on: another 1,500 yards of quayage.

Again things were much more peaceful at the South end, but East Salthouse shed underwent extensive roof repairs, a new shed was built at West Queens and part of East Queens was dug up for alterations to the railway lines. These would put about another 600 yards out of service, a total under maintenance of about 2,800 yards. It is not clear exactly which of these works were going on simultaneously, though clearly building a shed took several months. As a rough approximation we may probably accept them as simultaneous, because again there is no allowance for working space for the men or storage space for their equipment and materials, which were not trivial. This makes a tentative grand total of some 2.64 miles of quay out of commission, when the published lineal quayage of Liverpool was 24.1 miles, or 10.9%.

Bulk Petroleum Importation into Liverpool before 1930.

The pioneering stages of bulk petroleum handling and transport have been fairly well researched and written up for at least three reasons. They were obviously an exciting new technology, and the story of how petroleum stowage progressed from barrels to crates of square cans to large tanks mounted in the hold of a vessel shows just that measure of evolution from a primitive state which used to attract historians of technology. This pattern was then apparently broken by a decisive event, namely the placing in service of the first steam tank ship, *Gluckauf*. The fit of the narrative to the Smilesian template of how one told a story of technological progress was completed by the fact that the crucial innovation could be notionally ascribed to an individual, and a Briton at that.[128]

All petroleum handling was dangerous in differing degrees. Barrels leaked, sometimes considerably, cans could get crushed, tanks were left filled with potentially explosive vapour when emptied of liquid, as were tank ships. Because the distillation processes were relatively inexact in early years the precise content and flash point of a particular product might be only approximately known. The result of this was a considerable amount of research, particularly the work of Sir Boverton Redwood,[129] which was mainly published in technical journals. This encouraged and informed government interest in the dangers, resulting in both enquiry and legislation. Port authorities and local authorities made enquiries of their own, necessitated by the duty laid on them by the Petroleum Act (1871) to make appropriate bye-laws in their areas.

The third reason was simply the dramatic rate of growth of the trade.[130] This arose initially through the fact that mineral lamp oils were much cheaper than animal- or vegetable-derived ones, but as refining technology advanced uses began to emerge for a widening range of the fractions. The development of the oil engine, for example, first in semi-diesel form and then as a true compression-ignition engine, happened fairly quickly.[131] It did not lead to an immediately rocketting demand for 'gas oil' of roughly similar specification to modern diesel fuel, but it was widely adopted for driving barn machinery on farms during the agricultural depression of the 1880s and '90s. The Bolinder semi-diesel engine became popular in inland waterway craft and fishing vessels. From these successes, for semi-diesels had a much higher thermal efficiency than steam engines, it was clear to anyone who chose to look that the oil-fuelled internal combustion engine would sooner or later make inroads into the market for coal.

Conversely, in the inter-war years, there is little to catch the eye. The size of tankers did not increase greatly: vessels of 18,000 tons were in service before the Great War, and while the average tonnage did rise in the '20s and '30s, there was no runaway increase such as happened either earlier or later.[132] An 18,000 ton tanker was still considered quite large in 1939 and the first vessel to be dubbed 'Supertanker' was the *Velutina*, (1950) of only 28,330 tons. The growth occurred in the rapid increase of the number of medium-to-large vessels: at the turn of the century there were just over 100 tankers of over 2,000 tons; by 1920 there were 500 and by 1939 over 1500.[133] They tended to look pretty much alike from the outside and were unappealing to shiplovers, so few contemporary accounts of them appeared and this general drabness extended to the port facilities they used. Tankers were the forerunner of the so-called shipping revolution in that the discharge of a large vessel could be reckoned in hours rather than days (or weeks), so that speed of turn-round became a leading berth design parameter. They needed quaysides only for personnel and stores access, not for cranes, trains or high-stacked goods, so they did not need the quay to be wide, or particularly strong or even necesarily to extend the full length of the vessel. In Liverpool and elsewhere it was soon found that docks were not necessary if there was access to deep tidal water into which one or more T-headed jetties could be built.[134] These, like the tankers, did not make even engineers puff out their chests with pride. They were evidently regarded as cheap, nasty and routine: in the *Minutes of Proceedings of the Institution of Civil Engineers* not a single paper was published on the construction of oil jetties between 1919 and 1939. In the Mersey Docks & Harbour Board *Engineer's Commonplace Book No 5,* for the years 1909-28 there is not a word about the Dingle jetties.

The causes of rapid growth are not hard to find. The use of oil fuel for heating boilers had been carried on in a fairly primitive way in the oilfields in the 1860s, and the first US patent for mechanical atomisation of heavy oils was granted in 1868. This proved to be an idea ahead of its time, but the principle was refined into practice at, among other places, the Admiralty Experimental Station, Portsmouth, and in 1905-06 the ageing battleship HMS *Mars* underwent a major refit which included conversion to oil firing, the first large British naval vessel to be so equipped. Oil firing soon became the rule rather than the exception for destroyers.[135] The owners of the 'North Atlantic Greyhounds' remained aloof, the first oil-fired crossing not occurring until 1920, but the first sale of bunker oil in the port of Colombo was to *Oronsay* in 1910. Probably no great acumen was necessary to see that the petroleum trade was set to grow faster, but Thomas Newell, the MD&HB's Engineer-in-Chief was extremely confident. The oil trade was 'rapidly growing' and 'large areas of land will be leased to certain of the leading oil companies'. The growth in demand for fuel oil would be 'enormous in the immediate future'.[136]

Until at least 1900, the problem had been what to do with the lightest fraction, the 'petroleum spirit'. Some strange uses were found for it, including dry-cleaning clothes and (incredibly) dry-shampooing hair in ladies' hairdressing salons, several of which, along with their customers, suffered exactly the fate one might expect.[137] At some refineries it was simply burned off as waste. Although petrol use began to grow early in the decade, there are, perhaps, two turning points a little later.[138] The early motor car was a fascinating toy, but was so unreliable that there was a chance it would remain a toy rather than become a serious means of everyday travel. The fine engineering standards of the Rolls-Royce Silver Ghost of 1907 made it probably the first truly reliable motor car, albeit accessible only to the rich. The following year saw the introduction of the first volume production car, the Ford Model T, of which some 15 million were eventually sold: the Silver Ghost made motoring credible and the Model T made it achievable. If one wanted a longer term augury, that arrived in 1909 when Louis Blériot proved that aeroplanes were not toys either. Possibly the largest new demand was less readily foreseeable in that wartime developments in commercial and military motor vehicles led to very rapid peacetime growth of motor bus services and road freight carriage. Both of these employed larger and thirstier engines than motor cars, and used them for many more hours of the day.

The state of port facilities for petroleum importing in 1900

The importing of crude oil was virtually unknown in 1900, and the landing facilities had therefore to cater for 'petroleum products', refined at or close to the oil field.[139] With the partial exception of lubricating oil, each of the products posed hazards whether in bulk or not which required that the discharging berths should be as far as possible away from inhabited areas, or at least from areas inhabited by the influential classes.[140] Any buildings used for storage of petroleum in barrels should either be of a very high standard of fireproofing or built like an explosives works, in small units with strong walls and 'blow-off' roofs.[141] These requirements did not necessarily sit happily with the need to be able to transfer goods to road and rail vehicles. In Liverpool, for example, the first oil berths were at Herculaneum Branch Dock, at the extreme South (upstream) end of the Dock Estate and the first phase of the adjacent Parkhill Depot for bulk products had opened in 1891. It was not satisfactorily isolated, having the houses of Grafton Street overlooking the dock from the top of a small cliff, but to the south lay a considerable tract of land owned by the Mersey Docks & Harbour Board which, while not vacant, was inhabited by tenants-at-will who could not complain much.[142]

The Parkhill bulk facility was quite successful from the start: the dock dues on inward cargo from USA landed at Herculaneum, which is where Parkhill revenues were entered, rose from £1,134 in 1890 to £3,306 in 1895.[143] Thereafter the income dwindles, but that on incoming European goods rises rapidly, reflecting the inreasingly effective competition of Russian products,

especially from Baku. To this must be added the tonnage dues paid on the vessels: these are more difficult to separate out from the other trades, but were of roughly the order of an additional 60%. We may, therefore, hazard a guess that the annual marginal dues income resulting from the investment was about £3,000.

The cost of construction at Parkhill was met from the Engineer's revenue account for 'General Repairs, Maintenance and Improvements' spread over the accounting years 1889-90, 1890-91 and 1891-92, which raises some uncertainty as to exactly what was accounted where, but the total visible cost was £29,670. This indicates a return of 10% on capital, an unprecedentedly good result compared with other recent developments by the Board. It is, of course, too good to be true, for it takes no account of the cost of land acquisition, of which more below.

Herculaneum Dock itself was originally built primarily as a 'swinging basin' to serve four large graving docks and then it gained a long narrow branch dock initially intended for general cargo. Along the south and east sides

The Herculaneum casemates for petroleum in barrels, under construction in 1882. The trees on the skyline mark what was to become the Parkhill Depot, utilising the fall in the ground to two sides.

were the 'casemates', little artificial caves in the cliff, originally intended for the storage of dangerous goods in general, but later dedicated specifically to petroleum products in barrels. It was never a popular dock with the general trade, and in its bad years one large tankerful of oil would exceed the total tonnage of all other trades for the year.[144] If a place was needed to take a risk, this was probably a good one. On a more charitable interpretation it seemed to offer a quick turn-round, because it had its own large and comparatively under-used double half-tide entrance with about 27 feet of water on its sills at mean high water, and if the turn-round was quick enough the shortage of berth space did not matter.[145] Nor, of course, did petroleum supply exhibit much seasonality, though the demand for kerosene did.[146] The Mersey Docks & Harbour Board had installed tanks and barrel-filling and handling facilities at Parkhill to encourage prospective customers. This was an action of some generosity on their part as their normal policy was that any equipment peculiar to a specific trade had to be provided by the company wanting to use it. The location of Herculaneum, with its low cliff and sloping ground to the south, was particularly suitable for this stage of petroleum handling technology in that bulk kerosene could be pumped up to a storage tank in a single lift and then delivered by gravity for filling barrels or the little horse-drawn tanker wagons used for distribution to shops.[147] When, later, the question of filling railway tank wagons arose, the same arrangement still served well.[148]

The Acquisition of the Sites for Parkhill and the Dingle Terminal

From its inception, the Mersey Docks & Harbour Board was empowered to purchase land in the furtherance of the general objectives of the Board. During the 1880s, their attitude to these powers changed and they became much more acquisitive. This has been portrayed by Mountfield as a sage and far-sighted view, which on balance it probably was, but as he admits, there is also some

possibility that the purchases of land to the south of Herculaneum were pre-emptive.[149] That issue will be largely neglected here because the land policies of the Board in this period form the subject of another paper, cited above. The present question is whether the purchases made commercial sense.

The story of Parkhill and the Dingle terminal really begins in 1870, when a Colonel Freme offered to sell the Board a smallish 'country estate' known as Parkhill. It was no longer the desirable residence it had once been, partly through industrial encroachment and partly through the construction of working class housing nearby. The Board declined the offer, which was repeated in 1876 and 1878. Later in 1878, the Colonel lowered his asking price of £110,000 and, being rebuffed again, went to auction in 1880. The Board did not bid and the property was withdrawn after 'sticking' at £52,000. In 1883, the estate was offered to the City Council, who declined it, and later that year it went to auction a second time, being withdrawn at £55,000.

The Council was hanging on for a bargain price: they did in fact want the site, along with other adjoining land, in order to construct a huge new city abattoir. When this became known, there was furious objection from residents for miles around, because it was to be a vertically integrated establishment with its own tannery, glue works, manure processing plant etc. and they rightly thought it might be highly malodorous downwind. The scheme also infuriated the Board because it included a jetty, a clear indication that the Council was trying to 'steal' the coastwise cattle trade from the Board,[150] who now made it clear that they would oppose the abattoir proposal in Parliament and also became serious bidders at the third auction. Told that a bid of £69,000 had been received, the Works Committee recommended bidding up to £72,500 but the Board rejected the recommendation, increasing the sum to £75,000. The Council now attempted to do a deal whereby one party or the other would buy the land and they should take the upper part, the Board having the part with the water frontage. Had they not suggested that the Board should pay 25% more per square yard than they did, all might have passed peaceably enough, but they had waved a red rag to the bull, and later the same day a Special Board Meeting raised the maximum bid to £90,000. Any division which took place would be on the Board's terms. On 4 December 1883, the Board bought the land for £80,600 and on 1 February 1884 they entered into possession. But was the bull perhaps shown another red rag? It was noted that the Midland Railway had a representative at the auction, and the Board's suspicion, and fear, of large railway companies had a long history.[151]

It is clear that the Board had no immediate use for anything approaching all of the land they had bought, and even when the 1891 depot was built it used well under a quarter of it.[152] There were sitting tenants on the estate, with whom the Board made new agreements in March 1884. They also rented the upper part of the site to the Council for a temporary smallpox hospital at a rent of £50 per month. Notice to quit was not served until 1921 and the site was only fully and finally cleared for port use in 1925.[153] Buying land so far ahead of actual requirement was indeed far-sighted, but scarcely profitable. Adding the rental income to the marginal dues income estimated above and dividing it by the total cost *including land*, the notional 'profit' plummets from about 10% to about 3.3% Of the Board's debt of £16.5 million, £15.4 million was borrowed at 3.75% or more. The apparently successful Parkhill development was almost certainly, like much else in the Port of Liverpool at the time, failing to meet its true costs.

A similar situation applied with the Dingle Bank estate, formerly property of the famous Cropper family.[154] This consisted of some 18 acres of land with three large villas on it along with coach houses, stables and two 'ornamental cottages'. Offered to the Board and declined, it was offered at auction in 1877 and not sold. Serious negotiations with the Board did not begin until 1883 and on 5 November 1884 the purchase was completed at

£45,000. The title to this property had two serious flaws if the intention was to use it for port operations. There was a covenant on it that nothing could be built on it in such a position as to spoil the view over the river from the adjoining property of the Yates family, and although the Board's solicitor seems to have thought that the whole estate came with foreshore rights, these in fact extended only from the boundary with the Parkhill lands to Dingle Point. Foreshore rights to the rest of the frontage had later to be purchased separately. In 1890 the Board finally resolved both problems by purchasing 19 acres of land, formerly the property of the Misses Yates, from John Roberts MP, together with the foreshore rights of that land, of Dingle Bank and of a field known as Old Woman's Hey for £84,000 which the Board eventually purchased in 1919 for £52,000.[155] The Board had spent comfortably over a quarter of a million pounds on land which was yielding around £1,000 in rent.

One reason for this was obviously to prevent the Council setting itself up with a port operation, but another became clear in 1893, when the Cheshire Lines Committee promoted a bill to enable a link between its lines and those of the Liverpool Overhead Railway: the land which the Board owned allowed them to block a proposal of which they disapproved and which would have been harmful to the future development of Parkhill and Herculaneum Dock. Had they spent all that money in the interests of local control?

It would appear not: the Board had been aware of the potential of the petroleum trade since the early 1860s and they were obviously aware of the problem of finding space for the trade at one extremity of the system or the other. Surprisingly, in its upstream location, the future Dingle Oil Terminal had quite a good depth of water, indeed in 1874 the Herculaneum entrance was still the deepest in Liverpool. The rock 'casemates', for barrels, found a good and growing trade during the mid '80s and it was obvious that the next development would be carrying oil in bulk. There was another strand to the story as well:

for so long as anyone had kept records, the sandbank known as the Pluckington Bank had caused difficulty and expense at every dock entrance upstream of the Pierhead. The scheme was to build a training bank from Dingle Point which would (hopefully) produce a greater scour on the ebb and reduce the Pluckington Bank.[156] That was one reason why the foreshore rights were crucial and the other was that the intention was to build up the training wall to a sufficent height to backfill behind it. This offered the threefold benefit of reclaiming some useful land, conveniently disposing of a good deal of dredgings and gaining access to deeper water. The discharge of sand behind the wall began as soon as the wall was high enough to allow it.[157] The Board, in short, had strong reasons both negative and positive for its Dingle land purchases and their development would eventually place Liverpool as the third oil importing port of the country. One might, however, suggest that the

This view is almost the reverse of the previous one. It is taken from Parkhill and shows the original discharge berths, below and to the right. These later came to be used almost soley for bunkering (including coal provision on the East Quay, just out of the frame).

atypical policy of providing tanks, barrel-runs etc at Parkhill was an attempt to kick-start some initial business to justify the purchases.

It was an effective 'introductory offer', but reaping the big rewards would take time, because in Liverpool as in other major ports the initial investment had run ahead of existing demand and would suffice for a while. Between 1914 and 1921, world tanker tonnage rose from <3% of total world tonnage to >7%[158] and peace had brought an immediately increased demand for petroleum products and the means of handling them, necessitating investment in just about every port which wanted to continue in the trade. The first manifestation in Liverpool was oil companies wanting to rent land at Parkhill and Dingle Bank to build storage tanks and other facilities for their own use. The rate of growth in the trade seems to have caught even them by surprise, as the same companies came back repeatedly during 1919-20 for additional space. First in the queue was the Anglo-Mexican Petroleum Company, already tenants of No 1 petroleum depot on the Parkhill site wanting a modest 88 square yards to build a boilerhouse for process steam, but by 1 August they were back for 3,500 square yards, on 5 September for 27,887 yards and on 12 December for another 11,477 yds. The rent on all these plots was 2s 6d per square yard, so that Anglo-Mexican's dealings alone in the one year provided the Board with a new revenue of £5,369. One reason they may have come back so quickly was that on 11 July 1919 the Anglo-American Oil Co. had taken an extra 11,550 square yards. By June 1920 Anglo-Mexican had seven tanks built or building, the largest of them to hold 10,000 tons. In January 1920 British Petroleum and Anglo-Mexican agreed each to have plots of $3\frac{1}{2}$-4 acres at the now customary rate of 2s 6d per yard, or £2,117 pa for $3\frac{1}{2}$ acres. The Board's rent from part only of their purchases was now approaching £10,000 pa, disregarding the value of the strictly shipping side of the operation, and the customers kept coming back for more. Admittedly bank rate was very high at the time, but the Board was now approaching a reasonable return on its investment. No global figures for dues income for the terminal have come to light, and the rate of the dues rose and fell considerably throughout the period under consideration: a fairly typical rate seems to have been 1s 4d per ton for foreign inward bound, which means that dues of about £200 were paid on the contents of one 3,000 ton tank.

The Dingle Jetties

The greatest benefit of the original Dingle jetty lay in its small capital cost to the Board. In traditional shipping operations, an upturn in traffic produced calls for new facilities costing millions of pounds. The initial estimate for the Gladstone Dock system, determined upon during the anxious[159] years between 1902 when it was first mentioned and 1906 when it was enabled by Parliament, was a little over £4,000,000. A number of different schemes for catering for the petroleum trade were bandied around, including a dock and various jetty arrangements, but the one which was settled upon as the basis of the 1920 Dock Act consisted of two jetties, one for ocean-going tankers and the other for tank barges.[160] The estimated cost of the whole project was £81,000 and the larger jetty itself was completed in 1923 at a cost of just £16,514. This may be compared with expenditure 1922-24 on just one of the (admittedly splendid) new 3-storey sheds at Gladstone of £549,215.[161] Included in the £81,000 were improved road access from Dingle Lane and a new road across Old Woman's Hey. The necessary railway connection mentioned above was funded separately, aided by a contribution from the Unemployment Grants Committee. Owing to the 'pinch' at the south west corner of Herculaneum Dock, getting an acceptable radius there was quite a complex job: in 1923 £9,084 were spent on it. It was completed the following year, along with the road down to the jetty. The cost of the jetty per linear yard of berth space was about £33, a small fraction of that of a single-storey transit shed.[162] Expenditure continued on the same modest scale for the rest of the decade, with further railway improvements costing £6,639 in 1926 for example, and the purchase of a second fireless locomotive.[163]

The pattern of the trade is strange: numerically it was dominated by relatively small landings running up to 10,000 gallons or so and of these the great majority consisted of lubricating oils. Typically about twice a week there would be a fairly large landing of some hundred thousands of gallons and these were often of fuel oil. Less frequently, about once a fortnight, a really large cargo of up to two or three million gallons would be landed, and these were almost invariably of fuel oil.[164] There was, however, a considerable elasticity of demand for fuel oil: many vessels which had been converted for oil firing retained the ability to burn coal, and in 1922 there was a marked slackening in demand for fuel oil because the price of coal '…is so low as to make it the most economical form of fuel. Very little oil bunkering is therefore taking place.'[165]

The Works Committee now decided to press on with the barge jetty, and this was completed and opened in 1927. The following year the South Jetty was extended by 198 feet, making a total of 700 feet and approval was given to a further extension to 1,400ft which would easily berth two large tankers together.[166] The capital cost, therefore, of 'unlocking' the rental value of their lands was extremely small.

The South Jetty stood at some risk of being obsolescent before it was opened. In the first place, it was not capable of handling the largest tankers at neap tides: in September 1926 the cargo of the *G. Harrison Smith* had to be discharged into barges in the river.[167] In 1922 the first crude oil refinery in Britain was opened at Llandarcy, Swansea, and the Mersey's first opened at Stanlow, on the Manchester Ship Canal the following year. This naturally gave a boost to the importation of crude, so that as early as 1926, A. C. Hardy could write a chapter on oil tankers which treats only of crude carriers.[168] There was no question of building a refinery on the Liverpool side of the river because there was no suitable site offering large amounts of cheap land, deep water and seclusion.

There was also the question of what kind of petroleum product was wanted. Clearly there would be a strong and growing demand for ships' bunkers, but by the kerosene trade had suffered two technological blows. The first was the introduction of the pre-payment gas meter which allowed people not considered credit-worthy (ie the majority of the working class) to have gas lighting in their homes. The second was the municipalisation of electricity supply in Liverpool and many other towns and cities, resulting in the building of very large (for their day) power stations and a rapid fall in the price of electricity.[169] It would be a while before the poor got electric lighting, but it became almost universal in new properties.

Although the largest volume (subject to vicissitudes as mentioned above) in the early 1920s trade was in fuel oil, the most rapid growth was in motor spirit, initially transported, handled, and stored in the rectangular two gallon cans which are familiar to anyone who has visited a motor museum. In 1920, Anglo American began to establish the present-day system, of bulk delivery by motor tanker to a filling station equipped with storage tanks and petrol pumps.[170] Liverpool, like many other port authorities, forbade the handling or storage of petrol in bulk, and was therefore at risk of losing this valuable branch of the trade to its new rival across the river. The same year, the Board sought and gained sanction from the Board of Trade to charge higher dues for bulk petrol than for other petroleum products on account of the costly extra precautions required for its handling and storage. On 20 July 1920, the Works Committee recommended that construction of petrol tanks 'in the vicinity of the proposed jetty' be put in hand. Here again, as in the first stages of Parkhill, they were willing to invest to encourage a new branch of trade, and here again the results were successful. Such, however, were the fears both within and without the Board that the first bulk cargo of

'Dangerous Petroleum' was not landed until 1925. A pattern rapidly emerged of one or two fairly large steam tankers per week arriving with petrol, some of which was then loaded into coastal tankers for distribution, most of the rest departing by road or rail tanker.

In 1926, the arrangements for filling rail tank wagons were much improved by utilising, once again, the rise of the ground on the Parkhill site to put in two new railway sidings inland of the original connection and curving into the 'filling stands' which had been formed by cutting back the rock and using it as one side of a gantry to support the pipes, valves and hoses. This reflects the growing quantities handled: by 1927, National Benzole had two tanks, British Petroleum had 6 as did British Mexican, Shell Mex had two very large ones of their own and also rented two of the original ones built by the Board. The rest of the Board's tanks were rented to Anglo-American. In the midst of this bulk activity there remained a niche market for barrels: a drawing of so late as 1947 shows the cooperage on the Shell-Mex site, marking such details as the glue kettles and the bung box.

It is, unfortunately, extremely difficult to determine exactly how much money the Board was making from the petroleum trade at this stage of its development. None of the 'accessible' sequences of documents in the archive, has much to say of the trade, and certainly do not disaggregate its financial results.[171] It is not mentioned in Annual Accounts or reports. The Docks & Quays Committee, to which The *Weekly Returns* mentioned in Note 22 were submitted, did not even minute their receipt, much less their content. The Reports are scattered through the comittee support papers, which proliferated at around a ream per month, making location a slow job. Even when found, the *Weekly Returns* infuriatingly give the tonnage loaded or discharged, but do not give origins or destinations, so that one cannot calculate with any accuracy what the dues on a particular cargo or week's business would have been. Dock Dues and Town Dues on 'Oils, Class 3',

which included virtually all petroleum products, varied from 10d each (ie 1s 8d total) per ton for inwards foreign cargoes to 2d each for outwards coastwise.[172] Just as infuriating is the fact that the wages of the Docks & Quays Committee's employees, athough reported weekly, are aggregated, so one has no inkling of the labour costs incurred in earning the various dues. It is, however, safe to say that berthing at a jetty was a simpler task than manoeuvring a vessel through the dock system, so the costs to the Board would have been substantially lower than for a cargo liner of similar size.[173]

It is clear that in general terms the jetty was a fairly good earner. A moderate size tanker of perhaps 5,000 register tons would discharge of the order of 9,000 tons of petrol, worth roughly £750 in dock dues and town dues. This was excellent value for the Board when we consider the minimal capital cost of the facilities necessary to earn that revenue and the short time (usually between one day and two) for which the asset was utilised in the process. A general cargo vessel discharging 9,000 tons would occupy facilities costing several times as much per yard for at least three times as long.[174] This saving, together with the lower labour cost, was handed on to the customer, in that Dock Tonnage Dues (paid on the ship) were waived in favour of Wharf Dues at only 4d per ton, totalling £83 6s 8d on our notional 5,000 ton ship.

It was just as well that the jetty succeeded. The Board's financial condition in the early 1920s was somewhat daunting. It was not just that trade was slow in recovering from the post-war recession and then plunged into the great Depression from which it could only be said to have fully recovered in 1938.[175] In 1923, for example, the Board's debt stood at £36,273,332, the interest on which represented aproximately 41% of the year's total expenditure, and that at a time when several major engineering works were in hand. By 1927 it had risen to 46% and in 1930, by which time the new Gladstone system was fully in commission it reached 48%. Even when interest rates dropped and trade began to grow again, the position did not improve a great deal: 1938 was a very good year in terms of trade recovery, but interest still swallowed 41% of total expenditure. Without the easy money offered by the growth of the petroleum trade, the condition of the Board's finances would have been dire indeed. Yet to build the Gladstone system they had neglected other parts of the Dock Estate, especially the obsolete central docks used by the coasting and short sea trades, for decades. Major investment was essential, and that meant further borrowing. Had it been easy to do what I would now like to be able to do, namely separate out the costs and earnings of the jetties, it would have become clear that the Board's general cargo trade was in an even worse state than it appeared. In the circumstances the money needed for the large-scale re-development of part of the central docks, which began in 1929, might have been even harder to find.[176] There were sound reasons for not making the figures easy to analyse, notably the Board's recognition that the crucial objective of a port authority was to remain credit-worthy. Almost any mistake was redeemable except for that of losing the ability to borrow large sums at tolerable rates.

Conclusion

The purpose of this paper has been to outline a narrative of the growth of petroleum product importing in Liverpool once the pioneering days were over, and to place it within the context of the other trades of the port. The principal conclusion is that taking the next step —providing a meaningful quantified study of the growth of, and changes in, the trade will be an extremely time-consuming one. The work of tabulating simple costs and revenues, which in some cases was done for us at the time by the Board's clerks, for example for production in evidence on a private Bill or in response to a Government enquiry, is still to be done. It requires combining a number of intractable sources, in which process an authoritative apples:oranges conversion factor will probably be needed. Would anything worthwhile be learned? The growth of oil importing from a small and specialist business to being the largest single shipping activity (in tonnage terms) had considerable effects on the port services industry and forms, of course, one of the defining changes of 'era' in the Bird 'Anyport' model.[177] While oil importing on the Mersey fits the 'Anyport' model badly, it nevertheless brought about changes which we are at present ill-equipped to understand or interpret. At this preliminary stage, during the period covered by this paper it seems to have been highly beneficial to the Port of Liverpool by enabling it to diversify from its undue dependence on breakbulk general cargo at a very modest capital cost.

One interpretive point of some importance remains in doubt. Was the Board wise or lucky in that during its 'expansive' phase of property purchase it acquired the future sites not only of the Dingle Oil Terminal but also of its eventual replacement, the Tranmere Oil Terminal? It is clear that the acquisitions were made at least in part with a view to the need for increased facilities in the non-immediate future, and it is also clear that petroleum products were identified as a potential major growth area. What has not yet come to light is any positive link between the two—and it will be a hard thing to find, for announcing that one intended to use a piece of land for a petroleum depot would do little to facilitate its acquisition at a reasonable price. It was, like the absent statistics, something which the Board as a quasi-public body would probably not wish to have on the record. It is interesting to note that in 1946, when some Liverpool University economists tried their hand at forecasting the future of Liverpool's trade, the longest section of their report (70 out of 109 pages) was that on specific trades.[178] Nine trades were examined and among those which were not was one which now represents about a third of the port's tonnage. Oil.

Looking a Gift Horse in the Mouth: why the Port of Liverpool did not use 'free' labour on construction works.

There is a persistent local myth in Liverpool that some of Jesse Hartley's works were constructed by French prisoners of war, including his six-sided clock tower at Salisbury Entrance, which bears a prominent datestone reading 1848. The years 1815-1848 represent the longest peace between Britain and France for a couple of centuries. There were a few occasions on which prisoners of war genuinely *could* have been employed on dock construction[179]—and a number of members of the Mersey Docks & Harbour Board argued strongly for the use of German POW labour during the latter stages of the First World War.[180] Since Britain was involved in no major wars in Europe between 1815 and 1914, the scope for POW labour was very limited, but POWs were not the only source of 'free' labour. This paper sets out to find why it was that the apparent benefits of labour that came free of charge were accepted in Government projects but eschewed in commercial ports, taking Liverpool as a case study.

It was Gordon Jackson who first pointed out how profoundly irrational was the British government's lack of a policy towards its ports during last two thirds of the nineteenth century.[181] The port services industry invested some millions of pounds per year in the improvement or development of its infrastructure, and while the papers above suggest that some of the investment was ill-judged or excessive, it remains broadly true that without it British industry and commerce alike would have been powerless to remain internationally competitive, much less to grow. Yet this investment was effected by a motley selection of private owners, non-profit trusts, ad hoc limited liability companies, railway companies, canal companies, local authorities, bodies of Commissioners, parishes—indeed just about any form of combination of people except

government.[182] It was not just that there was no co-ordination of a national industry which might have been regulated in the way that railways were or nationalised like the telegraph system was: there was no apparent recognition of the fact that widely disparate ports, spread all around the coast, did in fact constitute 'an industry'. Not only was there no coherent ports policy, there was not even a suggestion that it might be a nice idea to have one.

Shipping was much enquired into by Parliament, and regulated in varying degrees of ineffectuality for most of the nineteenth century. Large volumes of legislation covered such matters as shipping finance, safety, tonnage measurement, labour issues[183] and the operation of cartels, suggesting that the neglect of port services was unusual. The Royal Commission which investigated the 'administration' of the Port of London in 1900 began with no clear idea of what a port was for.[184] Was it a commercial service or a public good? Should it be paid for in full by its users or subsidised in the 'public interest'? Nobody knew, and the eventual conclusion of the Royal Commission, that London should be administered by a new non-profit statutory trust modelled on the Mersey Docks & Harbour Board, was little more than a repetition of the equally inconclusive findings which had led, half a century before, to the establishment of the MD&HB itself. It mattered nothing that in London a Trust was to be an escape from the failure of the private dock companies while in Liverpool it had been the means of clipping the wings of an over-powerful local authority. Why, after all, need the answer be affected by the question? The *Return of Harbour Authorities*[185]—effectively the results of a Government questionnaire sent round by post—suggests that prior to that governmental knowledge of how many ports there were, where they were and what they handled had been rudimentary.

Shipping losses around the coasts of Britain mounted alarmingly during the 1830s and '40s, resulting in a swatch of Parliamentary enquiries into shipping and harbours.[186] Government funds were put into harbours of refuge at, for example, Dover and Holyhead, but long stretches of the east coast in particular remained devoid of adequate harbours of refuge. Harbours of Refuge, however, were a fearful financial millstone, because almost by definition they had to be large and to be built in difficult storm-swept places, yet they stood to be used only a few days per year. This burden could be lightened in some places by encouraging a measure of commercial use, as at Holyhead by the Ireland steamers of the London & North Western Railway or at Braye

Bay (Alderney) by fishing vessels, which at least generated a little revenue, though nothing approaching the interest costs of the work.

The fishing vessels provide another strand to the story: fishing vessels increased dramatically in both size and number during the second half of the century, but in nearly all cases their income was insufficient to pay realistic dues on enhanced port facilities. Yet fishermen held a special place in the affections of government for a number of reasons. They provided high-grade protein for the poor at a low price (and it is worth remembering that hake and plaice, for example, were then known as 'offal fish') and delicacies for the rich. At a time when Britain's security against other major powers rested almost entirely on an invincible navy, the fishermen were regarded as an important component of the reservoir of

The famous six-sided clock at Salisbury Entrance, said to have been built by French Prisoners-of-War. The quality of the masonry work, to say nothing of the chronology, makes this quite impossible.

skilled seaman necessary as a naval reserve.[187] Fishing was a major source of occupation and income in some of the poorest parts of the UK, notably around the coasts of Scotland.[188] One hesitates to suggest it, but there does also seem to have been a romantic consideration of keeping totally uneconomic inshore fishermen in work so that they could be quaint, spinning yarns for poets and posing for artists. In the early years of the twentieth century, these principles were acknowledged in Government improvement grants but nineteenth century mechanisms were different. However, something had to be done: the Navy needed safe harbours around the country not just for purposes of shelter but also to enable non-standard deployments in the event of any threat from an unexpected quarter.

In a rational world, at least two categories of people would have shared the Navy's desire for harbours of refuge, namely shipowners and marine insurers, and the three parties would have been got together to work out a joint scheme. This was certainly one of the aims of the *Royal Commission on Harbours of Refuge*,[189] but of course any such idea involved separating shipowners from their money. Not only would they not pay, they had already campaigned successfully for the abolition of the existing 'passing dues' payable to some East Coast ports in recognition of their function as harbours of refuge.[190] At a later date we find at least one owner willing to state quite openly that harbours of refuge were harmful to trade because captains would simply go and skulk in them when the weather was perfectly good for sailing.[191] Others took the view that they paid for insurance and it was the insurers who stood to benefit from harbours of refuge, so it was the insurers who ought to pay.

Crime and punishment

There was another way in which the Navy might be able to make progress, however, and it arose through national policy in penology being quite as vague as it was in port construction.

Primitive punishment of criminals around the beginning of the nineteenth century was simple and cost-effective: hanging was a reliable way of preventing re-offending and flogging, while less effective in that respect, was cheap and widely believed to be effective under either the retributive or the deterrent theory of punishment, especially when performed in public, although to some the abolition of public whipping of women in 1818 doubtless reduced the entertainment value. But even in the eighteenth century, there had been an alternative: British colonies which were short of unskilled labour might welcome transported British convicts to do their dirty work for them under conditions of what later became known as 'penal servitude'. When America got snooty about being used as a dustbin for the perceived refuse of British society, there was always Australia to turn to: as Michael Howard would have put it 'transportation works', because you probably never saw the criminals again. This was a comparatively humane alternative to endless hangings—and to unwarranted acquittals, as increasingly liberal juries would enter verdicts of 'not guilty' for the obviously guilty if the only sentence open to the judge was death. By the 1840s, parts of Australia too were becoming unwilling to receive more convicts, and by 1860 only Western Australia was still available, and that only for small numbers. The discovery of gold made transportation seem more an opportunity than a punishment—serve your time and then get rich—and the last convicts were shipped in 1867.[192]

A separate strand had been the development of a prison system. Prisons represented a major public investment, being expensive to build and to maintain, and they resembled ports in that while they offered several possible benefits in return for that investment, no-one was quite sure for which of them they were paying. They might reasonably be assumed to protect society against further crimes by their inmates for so long as they remained there—but eventually they came out again. It was possible to make prisons intimidating by denying convicts human company, sufficient food, sleep or daylight as well as by more positive initiatives like chaining them up and flogging them from time to time, thus subscribing to the deterrent theory. There were, however, some who thought that prisons ought to reform their convicts, sending them back into society with a corrected moral view of life and with at least some skills or knowledge to help them gain employment.

The idea of reform of prisoners became for a while associated with the idea of hard physical work, and the need to reconcile such work with the requirements of security led to the invention of the treadmill and the crank, where prisoners were required to carry out large amounts of physical work, initially for valid purposes such as grinding flour. Ideology took over however, and treadmills and cranks were installed working against a brake, where no use was made of their power output,.[193] This was clearly a blind alley in terms of moral reform and completely useless in helping discharged prisoners find gainful employment. What was needed was a form of work containable within the prison system which was useful both to the nation (as paymaster) and to the prisoner after release. It needed to be arduous and unpleasant, and because nearly all prisoners were uneducated and unskilled (and often pretty stupid, which was why they had got caught) it must be easily learned. It must involve minimal use of equipment, and that of a kind which prisoners could not readily break through stupidity or malice. Chronometer making was out, so what should it be?

'We are convinced also that severe labour on public works is most beneficial in teaching criminals habits of industry and training them to such employments as digging, roadmaking, quarrying, stone-dressing, building and brickmaking.[194]

These 'beneficial exertions' promised to provide a national benefit in the shape of cut-price harbours of refuge, for everybody knew that there was no labour cheaper than that which was unpaid and that dock and harbour construction involved a great deal of very arduous and completely unskilled work. There would be local spin-off benefits in providing enhanced facilities for fishermen at minimal cost. Here, seemingly, was a conjunction of interest made in heaven.

There was a further factor favouring this symbiosis. From the early 1840s onwards, civil engineers had been gradually accepting the merits of concrete for harbour construction, initially cast into shuttering as mass concrete, later cast in blocks and laid like giant bricks or laid as 'bagwork'.[195] All these techniques had one thing in common: they did not require the skills of the stonemason or even the bricklayer. They did not need men working in diving suits except, perhaps, one to relay instructions to a crane driver lowering blocks or bags into the water. Neither blockwork nor bagwork needed bedding in mortar: after placing the job could be completed by the newly invented technique of pressure grouting. These methods de-skilled harbour wall construction in the most delightful way, while requiring the movement, preparation and manipulation of huge quantities of heavy materials which were also difficult and unpleasant to handle.

In nearly all the plans proposed for these works the Breakwaters are designed to be of concrete in a monolithic mass... the manufacture of concrete blocks and the filling of large bags with cement are descriptions of work well-suited for execution by convicts.[196]

Here is another of the logical discrepancies which be-devil the story, in that those who sought to excuse what they characterised as the brutish behaviour of free navvies did so on the grounds that it was the nature of the work which brutalised the men.[197] How could the same work be bad for those who chose to do it and good for those who did it under compulsion? And if hard work was beneficial, why was it that there were more assaults on warders on public works than in ordinary prisons?[198] Just as nobody in government had really decided what ports or prisons were for, neither had they thought out the practical application of the work ethic in penal servitude.

One major pitfall lay in the suppositions mentioned above that unpaid labour was cheap and that navvies were unskilled. It had been fairly convincingly proven by campaigners against slavery on plantations in British overseas possessions that slave labour was in fact more expensive than the lowest grades of free casual labour.[199] The reasons behind this apparently counter-intuitive conclusion included the need to feed, clothe and house slaves regardless of the amount of work needing to be done at any particular time, the need for high levels of supervision and the need to prevent them escaping. All of these drawbacks applied to convict labour in this country. Then there was the question of skill: it was true that almost any fool could use a shovel, but it was certainly not true that he could match any of the output figures for proper navvies suggested by engineers who measured such things.[200] The less scientific yardsticks used for estimating the cost of excavations varied between 15 and 20 tons of spoil shovelled into wagons with six-foot side boards per man per 10-hour shift. That did not just need strength and stamina, it required technique, as did knowing how much to undercut a 'face' to make it fall without burying the cutter. A proper navvy's prowess at shovelling also depended partly on his diet—typically a couple of pounds of beef, a stone or so of potatoes and about a gallon of beer per day, and this the penal servitude system did not offer.

The result was huge discrepancies in the estimates made by engineers of the effectiveness of convict labour. The most optimistic was Mr McConnell of Chatham,[201] who claimed convicts could do $7/_9$ths (77%) as much as free navvies at pile-driving, but others prided themselves if they could get anything over 30% of the yardstick output for free navvies, and some clearly regarded the use of convict labour as a social obligation rather than a means of getting the job done more cheaply. John Coode, who became the acknowledged expert on the subject, found it 'difficult to say whether there will be any saving at Portland [harbour] by the employment of convict labour'.[202] This was a scheme on which some

1500 convicts were employed.

The disagreement as to the actual value of convict labour lasted a long time. Portland had required the construction of a purpose-built prison, and it was estimated in 1857 that the keep of the convicts exceeded the value of their work at, respectively, c£40,000 and c£36,000.[203] Yet the work at Portland, rough quarrying of rubble stone for the hearting of a huge masonry breakwater, was as suitable for convict labour as any harbour work was likely to get, except for its relatively high requirement for skilled stonemasons to add the facings— and their wages do not enter into the above comparison. Coode's opinion seems to have changed over time, perhaps reflecting improvements in the management of convict schemes: two years later, in a report on the proposed Harbour of Refuge in Table Bay (Cape of Good Hope) he was willing to recommend a combination of convict labour for the excavation with direct in-house management provided by a resident engineer, suggesting 400 able-bodied men would be necessary.[204] By 1882, with further experience at Colombo and elsewhere, he was comparatively enthusiastic.[205]

It is, however, not clear that anyone in the serious professional business of designing and building harbour works *ever* really thought that 'free' convict labour would save much money. Engineers were men who were paid to build things and to be successful at that they had to be as willing to run with contemporary trends as today's academic engineers do when seeking research grants. If convict schemes were sought, convict schemes would be delivered. There gradually emerged a consensus that a well-organised convict scheme might save about 15% of the total project cost and that on average a convict probably did about 30% of the work of a free man, though this varied considerably according to the exact nature of the work: convicts compared worst with free navvies at excavating and loading into wagons.

Convicts doing much less than half the work of free men nevertheless required at least double the supervision (not counting guarding), because they could never be relied upon to get it right—they were, after all, supposedly being trained to render them employable after their eventual release and their skills and motivation were usually minimal. There were many other disadvantages. The Engineer had no control over his labour supply, which varied not according to the number men needed on site but of crimes committed, fashions in sentencing policy and the physical fitness of the convicts. These were large schemes, often scheduled to last fifteen years or more, so guessing how many convicts would be available and what proportion of them would be fit for heavy work was necessarily an inexact business. For example, between 1848 and 1881, the total number of convicts in penal servitude fell from 3600 to 1525. Some of the larger schemes, such as Dover Harbour, were predicated on the employment of 1500 men at one time. Conversely, the Engineer could not lay men off if he had a surplus. There were quite sufficient ways in which large engineering programmes could run over schedule without adding almost random factors such as those.

The example which everybody watched was that of Portland Harbour, where work had begun with the new prison, completed in 1848. John Coode started here as a young man, working to designs by J. M. Rendel, and eventually became Engineer-in-Chief. Of the total number of men in the prison at any one time some would be completely unfit for such work (there were instances, for example, of men with only one arm being sentenced, somewhat pointlessly, to penal servitude) while it is clear that some of those officially designated 'weak-minded' or 'imbecile' were in fact certifiably insane and unfit for work of any kind.[206] The maximum 'effective' labour force he had at any one time was 1,100. The majority of the men reached an acceptable standard of fitness, but very few were 'strong and able-bodied', potentially capable of equalling the output of a free navvy, given

training and practice. This could be allowed for, but once again it was difficult to do so several 'generations' of convict ahead.

Perhaps the most galling thing from the engineer's viewpoint was the Ticket-of-Leave system, an inheritance from the transportation system. Penal servitude sentences were often as short as five years, of which convicts spent the first few months in close confinement in an ordinary prison, supposedly to meditate on their unworthiness and to resolve to mend their ways. They then went to learn to be quarry labourers, concrete moulders or whatever. A few learned the rudiments of a skilled trade, some as blacksmiths making and repairing tools for the others, others as stonemasons squaring coping blocks. There was no remission system in the modern sense, but convicts of consistent good conduct could expect to get a 'Ticket' early in the fourth year of their sentence. They were still convicts, but they were 'free' apart from having to report periodically to their local police. A surprisingly liberal reformatory provision, but what it meant to the engineers was that the best men they got were with them the shortest time, perhaps as little as 30 months, which was not long in which to learn blacksmithing or stonemasonry. Conversely, the least useful men were there the longest.

There were other limitations on the work of convicts. They were not allowed, for obvious reasons, to work in fog and it was not considered wise to increase the productivity of those engaged in quarrying by providing them with blasting powder. The site layout had to be carefully arranged to keep the free men working for contractors and the convicts (with their guards and their instructors) apart and this often hindered working arrangements.[207] Some necessary tools had considerable potential as weapons, particularly the navvy's traditional pointed cutting spade—which was so used in navvy disturbances. These and other dangerous tools had to be issued and re-collected with great care, though the risk was diminished by the fact that the guards were routinely armed with rifles.

These and other limitations on the Engineer's freedom of action resulted in a considerable secondary problem, that of keeping his heavy equipment, which could be quite expensive, working to full capacity, a feat which was rarely achieved. Coode considered that his tipper-wagon incline at Portland rarely bettered 50%, usually it was much less. Such things had a cost against them all the time they were on site, and obviously they remained on site much longer than would have been necessary with free labour. As with most other aspects of the job, predicting a finish date was almost impossible.

Perhaps the most 'integrated' example of the use of convict labour for harbour construction was Peterhead,[208] and it is notable that during the 'beauty contest' in which Peterhead was eventually successful in becoming the harbour of refuge for the north east coast of Scotland one of the factors mentioned was that the local economy would benefit from the arrival of the convicts. One might cynically assume that such gains would be confined to the local baker's sales of finger buns of suitable shape for concealing half a hacksaw blade, but in fact the locals were right. Having decided that 'Scotch convicts' should have the opportunity of benefiting their native land by their forced labour, HM Government now proceeded to build a considerable prison in Peterhead, albeit capable of holding only about 60% the number of prisoners estimated to be necessary for the harbour works, and that before allowing for the 'ineffective'—those incapable of useful work through age or infirmity, the 'imbecile' and those 'under punishment'.*

Their work was mainly to consist of quarrying, breaking up and transporting large amounts of rubble for the foundation and core work of the breakwaters and the mixing and placing of some hundreds of thousands of cubic yards of concrete. A railway was built to connect the quarry, the prison and the harbour works, and it is here that we see the first major problem with the scheme: this railway required a modest (by railway standards) viaduct, some 200 ft long by 27ft high: building it was skilled work which could not be left to convicts. As time went by it became increasingly clear that the ratio of skilled men to convicts was far higher than intended: it needed to be, and so it continued. Furthermore, the supply of 'Scotch convicts' proved consistently insufficient, which was scarcely surprising since the prison was not big enough and in 1882 there were in fact only 771 'Scotch convicts' in the country, of whom at least 25% would be 'ineffective'.

Any historian involved with projects of this kind comes to expect over-runs on cost and schedule: that is what civil engineers do. Peterhead may, however, have set some sort of record by making the first tentative beginnings of construction in 1885 and being still incomplete when penal servitude was abolished in Scotland in 1949. If completion of the job was the main objective then this would be incompetence of a truly epoch-making kind, but there is no evidence that it was. This was not a project like the infamous Burma railway, where the need was to get the line through: the need here was chiefly to keep the work going to keep the convicts occupied: it had become necessary for '…measures to be taken for employing the 1500 convicts… for whom… it will be necessary to provide disciplinary occupation in *some way or other*' [my emphasis] when the works at Portsmouth and Chatham Dockyards were completed.[209]

There was never the slightest possibility that Peterhead would pay for itself according to the normal rules of supply and demand. That had not been the primary intention, and one suspects that the wiser heads knew that, even as a secondary objective it would never be fulfilled. As it happens, they were wrong,

---

* The expression 'under punishment' is another example of the muddled thinking of the whole business. On the one hand the hard labour of mixing concrete was supposedly a punishment, on the other slackers might be 'punished' by being confined on a diet of bread and water. This did little for their capabilities when they duly repented and were 'rewarded' by being allowed to work again. Did hard work provide moral benefit or did it not?

but only through the discovery and exploitation of North Sea oil, a factor which we might forgive the men of the 1880s for failing to foresee. In the case of Dover it was openly stated that 'The primary purpose for the whole scheme is the employment of convict labour', and equally openly estimated that any income from commercial activity there would amount only to about 50% of the interest on the costs of construction.

The proposals for a Harbour of Refuge at Filey had been more ambitious: those pleading Filey's case saw that both Grimsby and Hull had invested in specialist fish docks, so there must be money in fishing boats and Filey could grab their trade by building superior facilities with convict labour and government money. What they were proposing was just such another venture as the London North Western Railway's hire of berths at Holyhead for their Irish ferries: the use of public funds not to generate new trade but to steal old.

The use of convict labour for harbour construction seemed a wonderful idea, beneficial to everyone. So it possibly might have been, but the decisions to employ it were taken without Government having the faintest idea of what it was doing. Gross over-estimates of the usefulness of convict labour, sometimes made in defiance of expert advice, were paralleled by a failure to understand the business of dock and harbour construction. We

might, however, do what government at the time did not do, and question what would have been the results had everything gone as they hoped and those emerging from penal servitude did so rehabilitated and equipped to work in engineering construction.

In the first place, there was a rigid structure dividing time-served tradesmen from others, and an ex-convict who had learned to draw down pickaxes would not get a job as a blacksmith, even less would one who could square a block get a job as a mason. This was not so much a matter of trade unionism as of class: skilled men came of good, provident, families who could afford to pay the premium for their apprenticeship and the foremen who effectively handed out the jobs were proud men who came of that class. They might, indeed, be paying a premium for a son of their own. It was not only what you could do, but what you were that counted. In this, craftsman foremen were naturally backed by their bosses whose jobs were similarly founded as much in position as in ability. So the rehabilitated ex-con could forget that avenue.

Semi-skilled work as a navvy was a better bet, but still not a good one. Navvying work had been plentiful and fairly well-paid before the collapse of the railway mania (in 1847-48) but after that supply normally exceeded demand. There were relatively good times, such as the railway branch-line boom of the

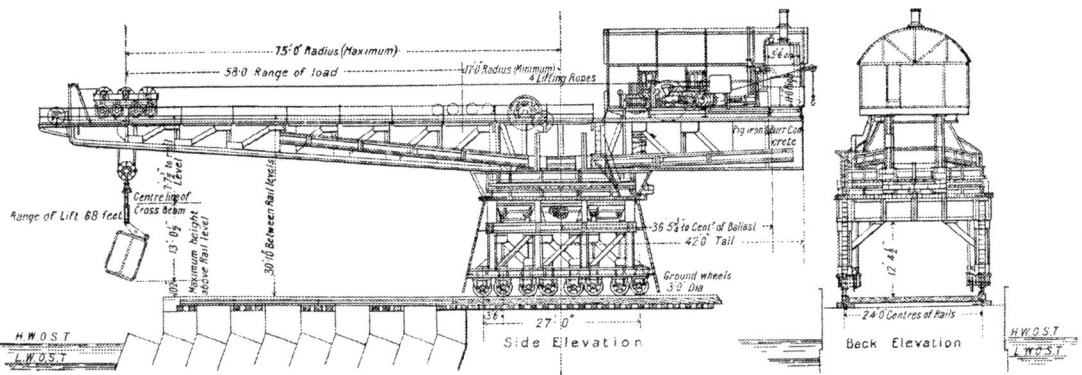

One favoured way of setting blockwork (or bagwork) on convict-built schemes was the Titan Crane. These very large machines made light of handling blocks weighing 50 tons or more, keeping plenty of convicts mixing and shovelling.

early 1860s, but more bad ones. Furthermore, as the market became increasingly dominated by a relatively small number of major contractors and a few big in-house operations, the problem of fictitious casualism arises. In some of the few organisations which kept records of supposedly casual labour it is clear that it was not genuinely casual at all, and that the same men were signed up again and again in a recognised order of precedence. In these circumstances we may well judge the prospects of the ex-convict.

Had he not faced these problems, had he been able readily to obtain employment, the result would only have been to drive other unskilled or semi-skilled men out of employment and/or bring about a fall in wages. In the 1880s and early 1890s, when even reputable employers were paying high-grade navvies 4s 0d per day or less, the burden would simply have been shifted back to the Poor Law Unions in a different guise.

If, however, convict labour was no solution to the problem of what to do with convicts, even less was it a solution to the question of what to do with ports. Like all the worst pieces of government intervention it had the effect of making government look both busy and beneficial, when in fact it was being neither. Over at least fifty years it gave the appearance that something was being done about ports, when in fact a vacuous ports policy was being subordinated to an unsuccessful experiment in penology.

Meanwhile, in the real world…

The true test is to look at the ports which did well in the mid-to-late nineteenth century and enquire whether they used convict labour: with the sole exception of Dover, they did not, and even at Dover the benefits were largely accidental.

The idea of the Liverpool Dock Trustees having thousands of convicts working at a snail's pace for decades is laughable. Jesse Hartley was a parsimonious man who would use re-cycled materials where he could, but he knew a false economy when he saw one.

When, for example, he started on the large (£1.4 million) programme of 'New North Works' under the 1844 Dock Act, he knew that the interest cost of its construction started when work started and the earning of revenue to offset that cost started only when the work was completed or virtually so and open for business. That programme was completed in four years, despite the fact that it began before the works under the 1841 Act (which included the Albert Dock Warehouses) were complete. In 1846 he had up to 4,000 men, some of them directly employed, others employed by contractors, on the 'New North Works' alone. That is more than the total in penal servitude nationwide at the time, and it needs to be multiplied by at least three to allow for the low output of convict labour and those unfit for work. The preliminary business of building a prison for 12,000 convicts would have taken nearly as long as the entire job as performed by Hartley's men and there were not nearly enough convicts to fill it anyway. Conversely, if every convict in Britain at the time had been sent to Liverpool, the works would have taken an absolute minimum of twice as long, (most probably more), that is to say the docks opened in 1848 would have been completed not earlier than 1852, by which time Hartley had completed Wellington, Sandon and Huskisson Docks, totalling some 38 acres of additional water area.

The difference in approach lies in the fact that the port authority knew what it wanted, it knew why it wanted it, it knew how to get it and it knew how to pay for it. Here, in the real world of dock construction, there was no place for confusing output with half-baked experiments in penology. From about 1840 to the time of his retirement in 1860, Hartley and his team were engaged in a frantic race to keep building new docks, each bigger than the last, fast enough to stay abreast of the growth in the number and the size of ships wanting to use the port, and they only just about managed it. The option of proceeding at a snail's pace, even if it had been significantly cheaper, was simply not an option at all.

Hartley has always had the (apparently justified) reputation of being something of a martinet. There is no possibility that he would have accepted involvement in a working regime in which he did not have absolute control over day-to-day matters, but it is important to remember that such an attitude is not merely the behaviour of a control-freak. In the working environment of a commercial port it was impossible to undertake large projects without the engineer having the powers necessary for him to discharge his duties, and in this the Works Sub-Committee of the Trustees backed him. The duties of Coode and others were not the same.

In short, unlike HM Government, the Liverpool Dock Trustees had a policy on dock construction, they adhered to it, they empowered their engineer to implement it and they earned their reward by being abolished by statute for being the largest and fastest-growing port authority in the world: in short, for being too successful. It is arguable that the new Mersey Docks & Harbour Board was a weaker and less successful organisation and that G. F. Lyster, their Engineer-in-Chief was not as good at his job as Hartley had been. That may be so, but he and they fully understood that, just as nowadays there is no such thing as a free lunch, so then there was no such thing as free labour for dock construction.

French Spies in Liverpool: A Source Essay.

Many historians deplore the practice of serendipity as a waste of time, preferring to work out in advance and in detail what they need to know, finding the fastest or most thorough method of finding it and then conducting a tightly-focussed investigation of the most appropriate sources. An appealing line of argument, but vitiated by the fact that we cannot judge what are the most appropriate sources unless we are familiar with absolutely all of them, and for many periods of history that is unlikely, probably impossible. The approach to research is with a partially closed mind—a small way down the road to the sin of starting out from the conclusion and working back to the evidence. One man's tight focus may be another's tunnel vision.

Archivists generally hate browsers too, not just because they cause work in calling from the stack material which may or may not be of the slightest use to them but also because the practice smacks of irreverence. How many times does one overhear a dialogue of the deaf along these lines: Q. 'Do you have anything about…?' A. 'What do want to know about it?'? The vagueness of the enquiry is unhelpful, indeed probably pretty irritating to one who gets asked it every day, but the reply is infuriating. How does the enquirer know what he or she can find out without knowing what is there to be found? Some archive offices give commendably full descriptions in their handlists, even including a few words of advice here and there about the usefulness or otherwise of particular classes of document, and some publish guides to the collections which give an overview to steer the visitor towards the most promising classes. Then there are those whose collections are on computer databases which allow keyword searches, a form of e-browsing. But there is still a significant residue of the other kind.

Librarians can be just as bad. They may be partly excused by shortage of space (and which library is not short of space?) forcing them to employ high-density storage unsuitable for public access, but that really should be a last resort because a library-user wanting a way into a completely new subject, or simply to follow a tangent, is unlikely to know where to start, and only in large and specialised libraries is it likely that the staff know enough of the contents of their collections to be of any help.

The two extracts here translated from the original French have never been cited or published in any work on the history of Liverpool, nor, I venture to suspect, have the books from which they come been cited in histories of any other British town, because if they had been they would probably have become a standard resort like Fiennes, Defoe or Cobbett and systematically looted for their authors' opinions of here, there and everywhere.[210] But I did not march confidently into the Archives of the Institution of Civil Engineers and ask to see either of these books because I expected to find something specific in them. I asked for them because I had found mention of them by accident while browsing in the old printed catalogue of the Institution's library and, having read some of Harris' earlier work on industrial espionage, wondered whether two Frenchmen writing books with titles like these at that date might not be indulging in a little industrial espionage, or, perhaps more innocently, technological tourism. If they were, it was scarcely likely they would not have visited Liverpool, and if they did they might well have something interesting to say.

I hope the reader will agree that they did. There is much to be said for seeing ourselves as others see us, particularly when the observer is both well-informed and highly motivated, as is the case with both Baron Dupin and M. Dutens. Charles Dupin was born in 1784, and his entry in *Nouvelle Biographie Général* runs to five pages of distinctly small print, indicating his status as a polymath, and before his first visit to England he served in the Corps of Maritime Engineers, and in the Navy. He visited England at least another six times in the period down to 1837, of which his most detailed account was in his *Voyages dans La Grande Bretagne*. That work has a very definite guiding theme, which is to find out the reasons, military, naval, technological and economic for France's defeat by Great Britain and her allies. As one might expect of a *Professeur Mécanique* in the *Conservatoire des Arts et Metiers* he was more convinced by technological and economic reasons than others, yet, as we shall see, his account seems almost negligent in terms of technology. His other publications were extensive and, in addition to themes suggested above, included works on geometry, siege engineering and fortifications. It is doubtful if such a man came to Liverpool for the sea bathing.

Jean-Michel Dutens was born in 1765 and after training at the famous *École des Ponts et Chaussées* emerged as a commissioned engineer-officer. He was sent to England by the French government to look at British canals, but his brief obviously got wider as the work progressed. In 1829 he published a history of French inland navigation, suggesting a broader knowledge of the subject than is exposed in the extract here. The latter part of his life was spent largely in publishing (and then defending, for they were pretty controversial) works on economic theory. He is clearly a less important figure both socially and intellectually than Dupin, but he is equally clearly acting in the long tradition of French industrial spies plying their trade in Britain.[211]

Dupin begins with a brisk explanation of what a wealthy and important place Liverpool has become in the comparatively recent past and drives the message home in his account of his second trip north by mentioning other ports which were, he said, almost abandoned.[212] He shows no doubts that this superiority of Liverpool over potential rivals centres on transport facilities, specifically docks and canals, the study and recording of which, despite the brevity of his account, he mentions twice.

His account of a trip on the ferry is a little gem. The boat he describes was the *Etna*, placed in service in 1817 and the first steam ferry to ply between Liverpool and Birkenhead.[213] Contemporary source material on *Etna* is rare, and while this account of her is regrettably brief, Dupin is the only passenger known to have set pen to paper. The information given is mostly incorporated in existing historical work and in the model in Merseyside Maritime Museum—with two intriguing discrepancies. Dupin explains how the chimney also did duty as a mast and could carry a square-rigged sail in the event of mechanical failure, whereas the model has a conventional mast and a bowsprit, not mentioned by Dupin. That, in turn, suggests that the vessel had a definite bow and stern rather than being, as Dupin describes, fully double-ended, including having a rudder each end, which the model does not. We move into the realms of speculation: the model's mast is shown centrally mounted, which means it must have been stepped in the 'platform', which would be a pretty doubtful arrangement, and furthermore the purpose of the mast is far from clear since there is no rigging for an emergency sail, not even a halyard for a fore and aft-rigged one on the forestay. There is no derrick, no masthead sheaves, not even a navigation light for it to hold up. With his already extensive experience of ships, it seems unlikely that Dupin could have been mistaken and equally unlikely that he could have been deliberately misled by some humourous deckhand having a little joke at the expense of the foreigner.

Harris, in his monumental study of industrial espionage,[214] stresses the failure of French industry, despite its spies, to follow Britain in the shift from a wood-fuelled to a coal-fuelled technology, and Dupin, for all his impressive credentials, still fails to recognise this as one of the reasons for Liverpool's impressive growth. He portrays the canals connecting with the Mersey as carrying raw materials to factories inland and then transporting their produce. At the time of his visits coal was a major traffic on most of those canals, but especially the St. Helens and the Leeds & Liverpool. Large heaps of Wigan coal could be seen at Clarke's basin at the end of the Leeds & Liverpool Canal and industries using coal in quantity, including the large Herculaneum Pottery, and the steam ropeworks which he visited, were conspicuous. Even more conspicuous was the steam machinery being used in the construction of Princes Dock in which Dutens rightly took a good deal of interest. Dupin's apparent lack of interest in it, and the lack of technical data on the *Etna*—possibly the first steam vessel he had seen—is, at the least, puzzling. Nor would affecting a gentlemanly *ennui* suit his agenda, which was to reinforce

the message back home that Britain's economic growth was leaving France standing.

His remarks about the counter-cyclical nature[215] of the 'work-making scheme' at Princes Dock are more astutely observed, but his description of what he implied are its effects, the growth visible on his second visit, are a considerable exaggeration. The only major construction programmes completed that year were Coburg Dock and an extension to Queens Dock, totalling together slightly less than seven water acres. Princes Dock was still far from finished, mired as it was in John Foster's web of corruption, and did not open to shipping until July 1821.[216] Similarly, his suggestion that the docks extend to 200,000 m² is misleading in that it includes land and quaysides: translated into the imperial measurements in which the docks were built, he gives an area of 49.4 acres when the actual water area was a little over 28. Surely our man has not just guessed the length and breadth of the dock estate and multiplied the one by the other?

One could continue, but it is not necessary.

*The model of the **Etna** in the collections of the Merseyside Maritime Museum.*

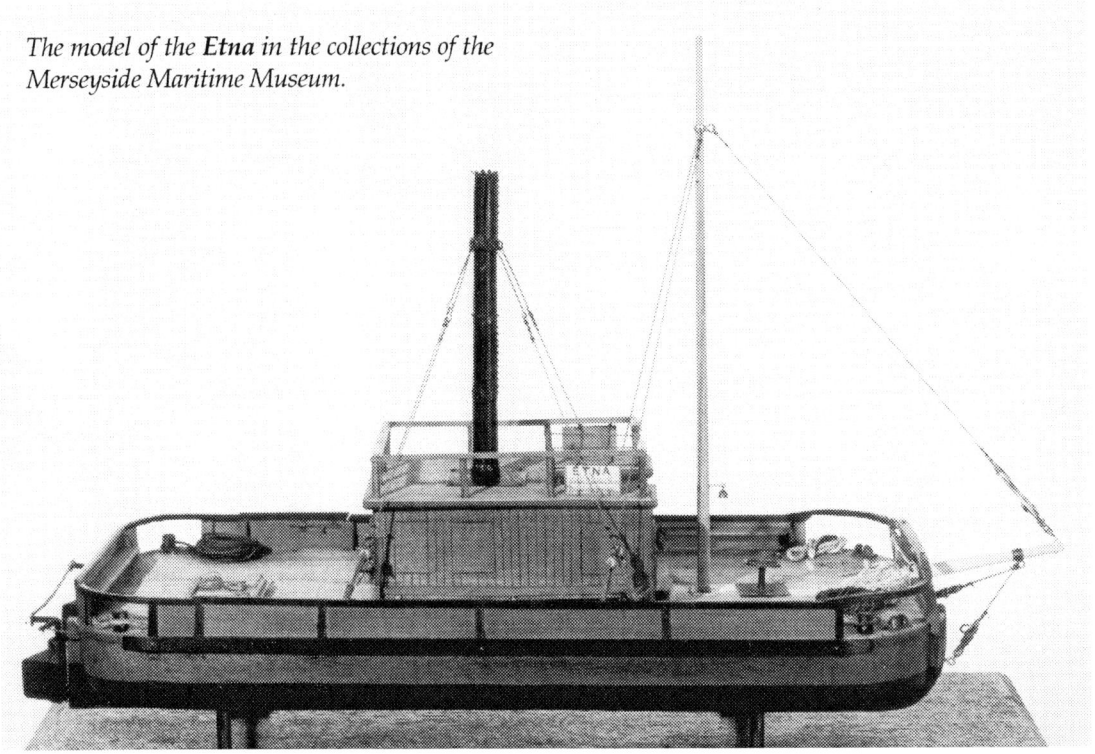

It is true that Dupin made copious notes and drawings of much of what he saw, but he chooses here only to allude to them, not to present them. That is because the book is not intended for his professional engineering colleagues: it is a work more of exhortation than of record, and as such is interesting, but scarcely to be relied upon in matters of detail. It also casts some doubt on the accuracy of his larger work, *Voyages dans La Grande Bretagne* (Paris, 1824) which one might say does set out to be a work of record. I shall not feel it necessary to suggest to the Curator of Ship Models at Merseyside Maritime Museum that he burn the model of the *Etna* as fallacious.

Dutens starts out in much the same way as Dupin by remarking on Liverpool's wealth, and like him, pictures the canals as important for industrial raw materials and products while failing to realise their importance in supplying coal. He fails to see the significance of the Old Dock in trade in addition to providing refuge and his enumeration of the docks is suspect: the only way one can get the total to eight is by

Part of one of Dutens' drawings, a plan view of machinery at Princes Dock. The steam engine (not shown) drove the long cross-shaft 'T', which in turn drove (from top to bottom) the limestone mill, the two mortar mills (only one shown here) and the winding drum for the waggonway. Clearly there must have been some form of clutch mechanism to engage or disengage the drive to the various machines, but this is neither shown here nor described in the text.

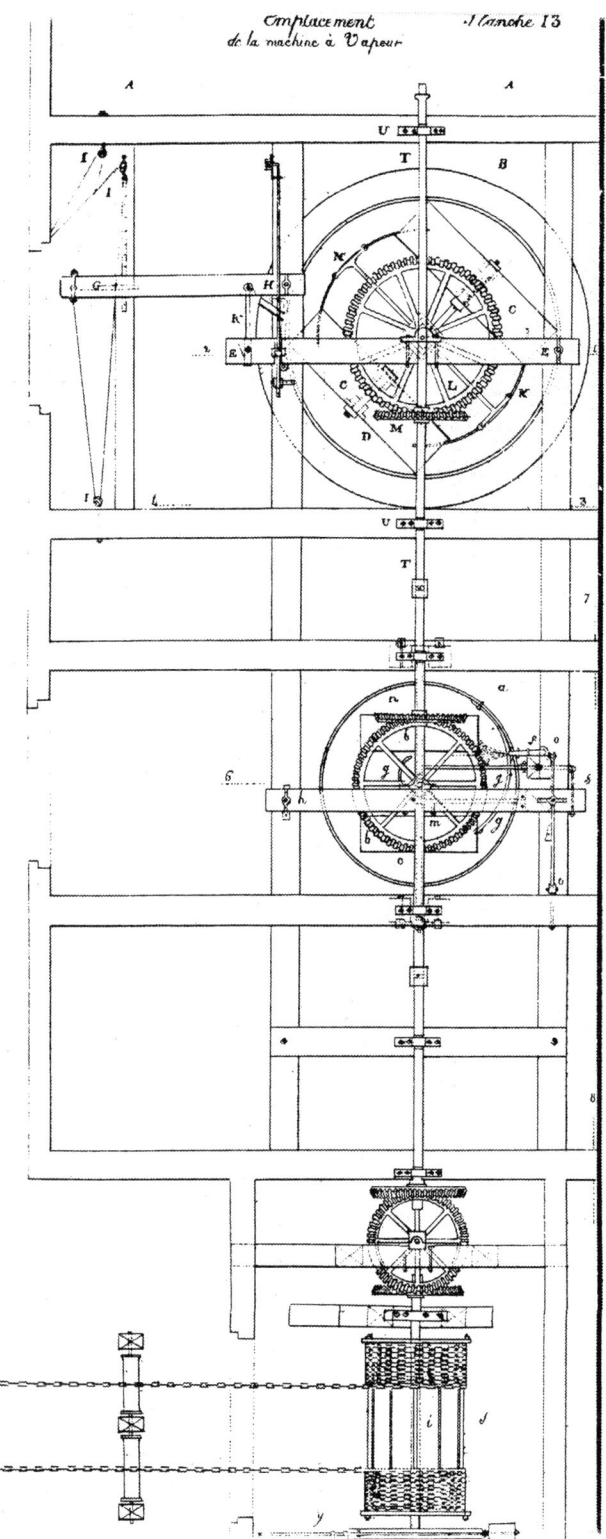

counting tidal entrance basins as well. Where he got the idea that there would soon be thirteen docks one cannot know, but the only works under construction at the time of his visit were Princes Dock and Princes [tidal] Basin which presumably count as two. The forecast that their area would soon reach 200,000 m[2] (just over 49 acres) was not achieved until 1830—and bears a suspicious resemblance to Dupin's figure. It is possible that they were both given a ball-park figure of 50 acres by the same inaccurate informant.

When, however, he turns his attention to Princes Dock, the quality of information suddenly rises. His statement that the works exhibited progress in the art is quite correct: Princes proved to be an extremely reliable dock in terms of construction, and he was not to know that certain aspects of the 'management' were deeply corrupt; it took the Audit Commissioners another five years to find that out.[217] The rate of expenditure, which works out at roughly £8,064 per month, £96,774 per year, sounds about right, but since the informant was 'Mr Foster Jnr'[218] (presumably William) we should not rely too much on it. The good quality stone he describes is that which came from Messrs Hetherington & Grindrod of Birkenhead, who were deeply involved in the corruption, but there has never been any accusation that their stone was poor.[219] In short, in so far as we can test out Dutens on things we already know from reliable sources, he seems at least as accurate as one could reasonably expect.

This is important for two reasons. The first is that descriptions of what actually happened on the sites when new docks were under construction are unusual for any period and quite rare in this one. In the specific case of descriptions in Liverpool this brief offering of Dutens' is by far the best we have. Even better are the drawings which go with it: virtually no working drawings survive which pre-date the appointment of Jesse Hartley as Dock Surveyor in 1824, in succession to the disgraced John Foster Snr.[220] Dutens' drawings show in sufficient detail that one could build a precision model, the

arrangement whereby the stationary engine which Foster had bought from Boulton & Watt on the advice of Rennie drove the mortar mill, the mortar mixer and the railed inclines used for spoil raising. It is a most ingenious arrangement of whose nature we can get no clue from other sources. While the mortar mill and mixer are fairly conventional, the 'railway' is really quite clever, employing double tracks and haulage chains which wind in opposite directions from the two ends of the same drum, thus raising one wagon while lowering another. For most of the rest of the arrangement, Dutens' description speaks for itself.

There is also a drawing of a double-leaf iron swing bridge, described as 'invented by Mr Ralph Walker'. Ritchie-Noakes attributed this design to John Rennie[221] who had certainly advised its adoption at Princes, and Foster had gone to Aydon & Elwell, Ironfounders of Bradford, to order the two bridges required for Princes. This was again on Rennie's advice, possibly because Aydon & Elwell still had the fountry patterns from the very similar bridge he had designed for the Wapping (London) entrance lock, erected in 1804.[222] If Walker *did* have an input to this design, then what is interesting is how Dutens knew. If we imagine him pumping William Foster for information, what answers might he have received to the question of who designed the bridges (which were not on site at the time)? It seems most likely that Foster would either mendaciously claim the credit for his father, or, more honestly, for John Rennie: Walker is not known to have worked in Liverpool.[223] In fact, Walker probably did not construct an iron swing bridge earlier than that of 1815 at East India Docks—a project on which he was Joint Engineer with Rennie.[224] But Dutens was not wrong: in 1800 Ralph Walker had published a design for a 'Double turning arch bridge'[225] indicating that, in addition to looking at things and talking to people, Dutens had done his homework as well.

The information on wages is useful as well, though in such an unstable economic environment we have no way of knowing how long the rates given applied. However, the decennial averages of wages in the building trade given by Skempton remain quite stable.[226] From the Dock Committee's Accounts, however, we can learn nothing of wage rates at this date, because there is a simple aggregated sum paid out for the year with no indication of how many men shared it. Even if numbers had been given, there were men working on several different bases of payment and at this distance in time it would be both difficult and unreliable to make an estimate. What is noticeable about these figures is that top craftsmen were getting paid only about double the rate of the navvies, whereas towards the end of the century the differential would be nearer three times at, in round figures, 12 shillings and four shillings per day respectively.

The originals

Both books are in the rare books sequence in the archives (as distinct from the library) of the Institution of Civil Engineers. They are part of the Telford bequest, and each is signed and dedicated to Thomas Telford by the author. They are in such strong condition that it was possible, with great caution, to photocopy part of Dutens' drawing of the machinery at Princes Dock. My thanks to Carol Morgan, Archivist, for her patience.

Translation of extracts relating to Liverpool from M le Baron C. Dupin's Memoir sur la Marine et les Ponts et Chaussées de France et d'Angleterre… *Paris, 1818.*

First Visit (Pages 48-50)

Liverpool, whose commerce is much less ancient than Bristol's, stands much higher in both wealth and industry and has seized the better part of the trade of her rival. The most amazing illustration of her prosperity is that just a hundred years ago, Liverpool's trade was only one forty-second part of that of the whole country, while now it is one sixth. Liverpool has thus prospered seven times as well as the average of a country which has

amazed us by the extent and rapidity of its general progress.

If we seek the causes of this unexampled growth, they may be found in her location at the seaward end of innumerable canals which pass through the most active and industrious manufacturing areas in the whole of England. So it is to Liverpool, which exports their produce, that manufacturers go to seek imported raw materials.

It was in Liverpool that the first dock in Britain was built,[227] which enabled merchant vessels to remain afloat at all times. The docks now now extend to over 200,000 square metres, about 4,000 metres lengthwise and 50 metres in breadth.

The best and most spacious docks are recently completed or still under construction. The severe commercial depression in England in 1816 has not caused work to stop. Rather has it given it a new impetus through a voluntary loan of half a million, used to employ the poor at the new docks during the winter of 1816-17.

Looking at the different docks, some older, some newer, the construction of their quays, their gates and their lift- and swing-bridges clearly shows the progress of the art of dock-building. I applied myself to working out what were the successive refinements which had been brought to these various constructions.

One realises that a great port as active as Liverpool needs large works-yards, numerous shipbuilding facilities and graving docks, workshops of every kind relating to maritime skills etc. I was an interested visitor to many of them, and I specially applied myself to recording how they differed from our own facilities of the same kind.

Second Visit (Pages 78-80)

On my travels through the west coast of England I visited several of the ports between Carlisle and Liverpool. They are almost abandoned: industry, ships, capital; everything has been swallowed up by Liverpool.

I have already described my visit to Liverpool on my first journey. I came to it again with a new interest, and after an absence of only a year I found a thousand new things. Enormous docks, only half-built twelve months earlier, were completed, filled with water and crammed with ships. Other docks were under construction, and quays and buildings of every kind seemed to spring up as if by magic. Trade, which had been so inactive, was flourishing again. This is how I found Liverpool on my second visit.

In Liverpool, as in Glasgow, there is a great scheme to light the whole town by gas, but the work is further advanced in Liverpool.

I visited again the great ropeworks where rope is spun, twisted and laid up by steam power: other ropeworks employing patent machines of greater or lesser ingenuity; a wonderful factory making high pressure fire pumps etc.

I crossed and re-crossed the Mersey on a steam boat made rather like an Indian double proa. Two identical hulls, long and narrow were arranged parallel but at a certain distance apart. On top was a large platform which carried the steam machinery. The paddle wheel worked in the water between the two hulls. There was a rudder at each end, to save having to change it over in order to go the other way. The smoke from the steam machinery escaped by a chimney which served as the vessel's mast and could, in emergency, carry a square sail. In the middle of the large platform which forms the deck of the boat is a cabin for the passengers, and there is another one for the machinery. Forward, aft and to both sides of the cabins, the platform is sufficiently spacious to transport sheep, cattle, horses and carriages etc.

I took another trip on the Mersey to the mouth of the Duke of Bridgewater's canal. There are three parallel basins, dug alongside each other, but in tiers, and with fine warehouses at their sides, then a flight of locks which climbs the hill. This system of works shows what can be achieved by the wealth, industry and spirit of enterprise of a single individual driven by a noble love of the public good.

Leaving Liverpool for the last time, I went to Chester…

*Extract relating to Liverpool from J. Dutens, **Memoires sur les Travaux Publics d'Angleterre,** 2 Vols, Paris, 1819, Vol 2.*

Port of Liverpool.

The rapid rise to prosperity of the rich and beautiful town of Liverpool has several causes: her position at the mouth of the Mersey; her remoteness from London, which cannot fail to leave to her a great part of the general commerce between England and her colonies and with foreign countries; her relative closeness to Leeds and even to Hull, her proximity to Chester and, above all to Birmingham, Manchester and Lancaster.[228] By means of the Leeds & Liverpool, Ellesmere, Trent & Mersey, Bridgewater, Lancaster and Douglas[229] Canals these three manufacturing towns send the fruits of their industry and their laborious midnight toil to Liverpool, there to exchange them for the coarse products and raw materials they receive from America and other parts of the world.

In the reign of Queen Anne, Liverpool constructed a dock to shelter storm-tossed vessels: she now has eight of them, and will soon have thirteen, not counting the extensions of the older ones, which will have a total area of 200,000 square metres.

The works which are now going on for the dock called the Regent's Dock [Princes Dock], which is to be 500 yards (457 metres) long by 110 yards (100 metres) wide, are being carried out with great skill by Mr. Foster. One finds in the way they are managed that same progress in the art whose benefits I remarked upon at the ports of Chatham and Plymouth. They are spending 200,000 francs a month on the work at Liverpool.

The materials used in the works are of the finest quality. The freestone, a dense and very homogeneous sandstone, comes from quarries on the opposite coast [of the Mersey], only one and a half leagues away.[230]

In their foundation work they make extensive use of a mortar invented by Messrs

Parker and Wyat [sic] of London, known in England as Roman Cement. This cement is made up of one part volcanic rock from the Isle of Sheppey, two [Metric] leagues from Sheerness, which is burned and ground like limestone; one part limestone and two parts of sand.The proportions are varied according to the nature of the work.

The workmen are served by a system of railways, some built on the level and some on inclined planes. Mr Foster Jnr. told me that their total length was no less than three miles. (4872 metres.) These railways are made like all the others, with a bar 14 centimetres wide and an upstand or raised edge to restrain the wagons, and about a metre long. These bars are layed on transverse timbers. They cost, including those parts requiring points or turntables, ten shillings per yard run, or 13.52 francs per metre. That amounts to a total of 65,261.04 francs, which is not a great expense when one takes into account that the components of these railways will last more or less for ever, and besides, they suffer only a very slight diminution in their weight and hence their value.

The whole of this working system is driven entirely from one point, by a single motive power, the steam engine. The engine is set up on the level ground between the basin and the Regent's Dock, and works the pumps, grinds the limestone and mixes the mortar with three mills. It also drives the two wagons on a double railed incline, lowering construction materials and raising spoil and, finally, it drives several cranes for lifting materials. Plate 13 gives a general plan of the arrangement of these machines.

Immediately behind the frame of the steam engine is the shed containing the mill B, which grinds the limestone, by means of the two mill wheels CC, driven by a double motion from the fixed platform D and two others A', of which only one is shown, are used for mixing the mortar by means of the two wheels BB' which move on their own on a revolving platform C'. Beyond the first shed is a second one, containing the drum S' on which the

chains connected to the wagons T' are wound and unwound. These wagons move in opposite directions, one ascending while the other descends, on the inclined place U'U'.

The wagons, rising or descending on the inclined plane arrive on a pivoted bridge X' placed at the top of the incline and by turning the bridge a quarter turn they can be placed in the desired position, whether to move onto the incline or to the place where they are to be loaded with stone for the construction work or to discharge the spoil which has been cut and raised.

Quite separately from this incline, which is driven by the steam engine, there is another whose wagons are moved by a double winding drum worked by hand: this drum, which is extremely strongly constructed, works in the same manner as at the port of Coal-Port, below the Hay Incline, which we illustrated in Plate 4, except that it is made up of two sections of drum on which the chains roll and unroll, and the brake wheel is situated in the middle.

As we remarked at the beginning of this account, the government, which only takes on the construction of naval ports, as part of those means of national defence which must remain in its hands, leaves it to the spirit of industry, of commerce and of the speculations of the merchants to look after the operations of the commercial ports, by means of granting them the right to levy dues on ships using such ports.

The works at the port of Liverpool being the most interesting among all the commercial ports, and those which are carried out under the most recent Acts of Parliament, (the latest of these Acts dating only from 1811) I have thought fit, from choice, to take their method of management as an example, to give an idea of the way in which the works in other ports are generally being pushed into the background. Hence I give, in the notes which follow this memoir, an account of the Acts under which the various works at Liverpool have been constructed, the rates of Dock Dues which apply and the regulations governing its management and its police which are actually in force.[231]

Notes.

It will be much easier for the reader to understand if I give the day rates of the workmen on these great works: according to information given me by Mr Foster Jnr, they are as follows:

Stone cutters	3s 6d (4.43F)
Stone setters	4s 2d (5.17F)
Mason's labourers	2s 6d (3.10F)
Master carpenters	4s 2d (5.17F)
Journeymen	3s 8d (4.54F)
Price of a cubic foot of wood	3s 2d (3.93F)

The excavation work is done on a piece work basis by workers who cannot usually earn more than 12 shillings (14.88F) per week.

Conclusion

As we have seen, both Dupin and Dutens were well-informed observers, and it is perhaps surprising that they made so many mistakes, especially Dupin, whose distinguished *Curriculum Vitae* would lead us to expect better. Visiting Liverpool at a time when it was just taking off into its period of fastest growth must have been a depressing experience for both of them. Applying Harris' notion of technological debtors or creditors, they came to look at the port and the canals as debtors. A century before, the boot had been entirely on the other foot. Vauban's work fortifying Dunkirk in the late 1670s had included building a wet dock of considerable size to provide safe all-year-round moorings for warships, and it is not impossible that Thomas Steers, the Engineer of Liverpool's first dock, had seen it during his time as an Army Quartermaster serving in the Low Countries. A mightier work still was the *Canal du Midi*, opened in 1685, with cuttings, embankments, flights of locks and a huge summit-level dam to provide the water supply. Works like the Trent & Mersey, mentioned specifically by Dutens and implicitly by Dupin, arose at least in part from the Duke of Bridgewater's time spent examining the *Canal du Midi*. They came decades later and were of pigmy size compared with Pierre-Paul Riquet's masterpiece.

Both writers draw a wrong message from what they found, that the strength of Britain, as exemplified by the prosperity of Liverpool, arose to a noticeable extent from the fact that, in contrast to France, British transport infrastructure was 'privatised'. In many ways British infrastructure would have been better nationalised: canals, ports and railways all in turn undertook wasteful developments in the competition for trade. The only canal in Britain which will bear any comparison with the *Canal du Midi* as an engineering feat is the Caledonian, which was effectively a central government project.[232] Had Pierre-Paul Riquet been transposed into the British system of construction by joint stock companies he would have been patronised as a daydreamer. The Trent & Mersey indicates the kind of canal you got when there were shareholders to keep happy. It was built on the cheap: shallow, winding and allowing a maximum boat width of only seven feet to keep down the cost of excavation and lock construction; locks strung out at irregular intervals instead of grouped in flights;[233] locks of differing height (which wasted water)—one could go on, but one of the things the French had come to see was an excellent example of how not to build a canal.

They did not look at (or if they did, they did not mention) the St Helens Canal. Only eight miles long at the time, (albeit extended later) it claimed the title of the 'world's first industrial canal'. The *Canal du Midi* was built partly for strategic and partly for agricultural reasons: there was no industry in the region for it to serve, nor any natural resources which would encourage industry to develop there. That much both writers recognise with respect to Liverpool, with their mentions of the canals connecting with the industrial hinterland. What they have not grasped is that Liverpool is a symptom and a symbol of a new type of economy, one where many former constraints can be eliminated by the use of coal. It was no longer necessary to locate an industry where there was water power available, nor was it necessary to stop work when it went dark: coal gas would solve the problem. One no longer needed a favourable wind to cross the Mersey: steam would do the work, and it was not long before steam ferries became powerful enough to go against the tide as well as the wind. The year after Dutens went to press the first proposal for a steam railway to Manchester was made public.

The factual information in these two extracts is interesting and useful, but scarcely of great importance. What is perhaps important, however, is that two skilled professional observers largely failed to answer the question 'what went wrong in France?'

because they did not correctly identify what was going right in England. At a local level, this might perhaps cause us reflect on the entrepreneurial talents upon which Dutens remarks as funding the port infrastructure. They had also made Liverpool 'rich and beautiful' and would very soon make it much richer, though the arrival of James Muspratt's chemical factory in 1822 would do little for its beauty. They understood, as the French did not, the way in which all the factors mentioned above, and many more, interacted with each other to produce an economic system which was qualitatively as well as quantitatively superior.

Notes.

1 Certanly there was nothing wrong with its labour efficiency: in June 1930, for example, it discharged cargoes at the average rate of 17.8 tons per gang, while King George V Dock, London managed only 12.18.

2 This episode is investigated in my 'Land Policies in the Port of Liverpool 1709-1857', *International Journal of Maritime History*, XII (2000), pp69-84.

3 Discussed by the Traffic Committee on 16 April 1928.

4 An earlier version of this paper was presented to the 'Steam at Sea' conference held at Hull in 1996

5 For further details see, for example, G. Jackson, *History & Archaeology of Ports*, Tadworth, 1983; A. Jarvis, *The Liverpool Dock Engineers*, Stroud, 1996.

6 For sailing packets see R. G. Albion, *Square Riggers on Schedule*, Princeton, 1938; for paddle steamers, N. R. Bonsor, *North Atlantic Seaway*, Jersey, 1978.

7 The intermediate Cunarders *Ivernia* and *Saxonia* (1899), for example, drew 32ft fully laden: E. W. de Rusett, 'Recent Developments in Cargo & Intermediate steamers', *Minutes of the Proceedings of the Institution of Civil Engineers*, (*Min Proc ICE*), CLVIII (1903-04), pp156-84, at p159.

8 I have excluded the large and powerful bucket ladder dredgers which, in the latter part of the century, were probably used more for construction or 'deepening and underpinning' jobs than they were for maintenance.

9 For the history of Albert Dock see N. Ritchie-Noakes, *Liverpool's Historic Waterfront*, London, 1984; A. Jarvis & K. Smith (eds), *Albert Dock: Trade and Technology*, Liverpool, 1999. For a general account of the chief innovations in hydraulic engineering, I. McNeil, *Hydraulic Power*, London, 1972.

10 But only initially: casualism soon crept in and spread.

11 T. Smith, 'Hydraulic Power' in R. J. M. Carr (Ed) *Docklands*, London, 1986, at p161. *G. F. Lyster's Commonplace Book* gives the number of hydraulic appliances at the three warehouse

docks as 368, while there were only 15 hydraulic cranes in the whole of the rest of the Liverpool system.

12 Smith, *op cit*, p164.

13 For high, even excessive, speed of discharge by ships' tackle, see Jarvis, *Dock Engineers*, pp170-71.

14 *Engineer's Report* 1859.

15 The Engineer's Department carried out a careful series of tests to compare the performance of hand and hydraulic machinery, recorded in the *Commonplace Book* No.1, 1866, p49.

16 The first hydraulic-powered entrance gates were not at Liverpool but at the Royal Docks, Grimsby, completed in 1852 and formally opened in 1854, but with only a 70ft passage to close they were considerably smaller than those at Canada

17 For much of the second half of the nineteenth century there were sporadic disputes over rating valuation between MD&HB and the various local authorities. These generated the sequence of *Machinery Lists*, available on microcard in the *Merseyside Dockland Survey* collection. They give convenient brief details of hydraulic machinery, often including both the date of installation and the original cost.

18 E. Clark, 'The Hydraulic Lift Graving Dock', *Min Proc ICE*, XXV (1865-66), p300 *et seq*, describes a lift built for the Victoria Docks Co. (London) which, at that comparatively early date, had a lifting capacity of 5,870 tons weight

19 The *Machinery Lists*, although not very standardised in form often give engine or boiler sizes. Armed with a contemporary engineer's pocket book, one can roughly deduce either from the other. (because boiler pressures were pretty standard according to size, type and approximate date.) A larger number of smaller boilers was preferable for maintenance purposes to a smaller number of larger ones.

20 *Worked-up Paper* 100 gives the estimated coal requirements of all the Board's plant, as issued to those wishing to tender to supply. No convenient record has yet come to light

showing how much they actually burned per year or what it cost.

21 The Board periodically published a *Tabular Statement* of the dimensions of docks in service at the time. That for 1874, for example, shows Herculaneum Graving Docks as the deepest, 4ft below Old Dock Datum: Herculaneum Entrance was 8ft below.

22 For the inadequacies of the works under the 1873 Dock Act (of which these were part) see A. Jarvis, 'G. F. Lyster and the Role of the Dock Engineer', *The Mariner's Mirror*, 78 (1992), pp179-99.

23 This was the subject of some acrimonious letters to the local press in 1883, eg *Liverpool Courier* 7 May, 28 August.

24 The 'Birkenhead Lobby' was still active and objected stridently to the 1872 Bill and the coasting trade objected to continued heavy expenditure on facilities for large vessels, when, they understandably felt, facilities for coasters were neglected.

25 The 'bucketting engine' was just that: a self-acting hydraulic lift which filled a large bucket with water, lifted it and then emptied it into a spillway. Its replacement by a chain pump is mentioned in the *Engineer's Report* for 1884.

26 These proceedings are documented in *Unbound Worked-up Paper* G13bPt 2.

27 There is a good account of this machinery in *Fairplay*, 20 March 1886.

28 It had a long gestation: it seems fairly clear that Denis Papin built functioning centrifugal pumps in the 1690s: see L. E. Harris, 'Some factors in the early development of the centrifugal pump', *Transactions of the Newcomen Society* XXVIII (1951-52), pp187-202.

29 D. Thomson, 'Centrifugal Pumps', *Min Proc ICE* XXXII (1870-71), pp 26-64; J. Abernethy, 'Description of works at the Ports of Swansea, Blythe and Silloth', *ibid* XXI (1861-62), pp309-44; E. H. Clark, 'Great Grimsby Docks', *ibid*, XXIV (1864-65), pp38-61; T. Hawthorn, 'Docks & Warehouses at Marseilles' *ibid*, pp144-67.

30 The Royal Commission for Historic Monuments in England, *Survey of London*, Vol XLIII, p366.

31 *ibid*, p370; J. &. H. Gwynne, *Notes on Centrifugal Pumping Machinery*, London, 1885, p2.

32 *Fairplay, loc cit.*

33 Some figures illustrating the benefits may be found in the next paper.

34 *Engineering*, 26 December 1890, p755.

35 No systematic record of coal consumption has yet come to light. ENG/2/7 is one of a number of isolated documents which give figures: in this case an average monthly consumption of 518 tons per station in 1909.

36 This issue is considerd in more detail in paper 3, below.

37 *Clarence Graving Dock Stores and Log Book*, ref SAS/19/B/6/19.

38 *Machinery Lists*, North Series No. 9

39 H. F. Cornick, Vol. 3, pp132-33.

40 RCHME *op cit*, p326; Dock Committee Minutes, 2 July 1811. J. Dutens, *Memoires sur les Travaux Publiques de France et d'Angleterre*, 2 Vols, Paris, 1819. In Volume 2 is a better description of the works at Princes than any found in English sources. (See the source essay at the end of this collection.)

41 For more on spoil handling, see Jarvis *Dock Engineers*, Chapter 6. Not all engineers agreed with the cube relationship: F. Hudleston, in a contribution to the discussion of H. H. West, 'The Tonnage Laws and the Assessment of Harbour Dues & Charges', *Min Proc Ice*, CLVII (1903-04) at p23 claimed that excavation costs were much the same at 30ft as at 20ft and that masonry costs increased roughly as the square.

42 C. Andrews, 'The Somerset Dock at Malta', *Min Proc Ice*, XXXIII (1871-72) pp352-75.

43 For a wide selection of illustrations of different retaining wall sections, see P. N. Bray & P. F. B. Tatham, *Old Waterfront Walls*, London, 1992, pp23-62.

44 G. F. Lyster gave an account of this in his evidence before the *Select Comittee to Enquire into Schemes by Local Authorities for Providing Electricity*, British Parliamentary Papers 1878-9 (224) XI.375.

45 B. Cunningham, *Dock Engineering*, London, 1906, pp78-79.

46 This situation produced the interesting technological freak *Atlas*, Cory's hydraulic coaling pontoon, of which a model may be seen in Merseyside Maritime Museum.

47 For further information on Bramley-Moore see A. Jarvis, *Liverpool Central Docks 1799-1914*, Stroud, 1991, pp100-116.

48 The imprecision of this statement results from the fact that the Board's different coaling facilities were each chiefly associated with one particular area of supply. Contrary to popular belief, shipping companies did not necessarily develop and maintain a preference for a

particular kind of coal. While Holt's ships, sometimes nicknamed 'The Welsh Navy', tended to stick to Best Welsh, surviving Engineer's Logs from Cunard reveal the use of a wide variety of types. These variations in source were reflected by variations in traffic at the different coal berths, eg West Yorkshire steam coal was handled mainly at Bramley-Moore, North Wales mainly at Birkenhead.

49 The Board rarely worked such things out. For some retrospective analysis, see 'Think Big? Returns on Different Scales of Investment…' in this collection.

50 Worked-up Paper 4/2 contains several references to this process, from December 1905 onwards.

51 An earlier version of this paper was presented at a seminar held during at the Association for the History of the Northern Seas Conference, Liverpool, 2001.

52 G. Jackson, *The History & Archaeology of Ports*, Tadworth, 1983, pp116-17.

53 A. Jarvis, 'The Port of Liverpool and the Shipowners in the late nineteenth century', *The Great Circle* 16 (1994), 1-22.

54 Milford was a particularly sad case, where a large investment programme was completed in 1888 to enable the port to handle large oceanic trades: it ended up handling fishing boats.

55 The re-use of the names Toxteth and Harrington does not indicate that these were mere extensions of the earlier docks of those names. The 1841 Toxteth Dock was a miserable little privately-owned tidal basin and the 1839 Harrington Dock was no more impressive. For details see N. Ritchie-Noakes, *Liverpool's Historic Waterfront*, London, 1984, p67.

56 Except, of course, for the *Great Eastern*, which was skilfully designed to be unable to enter any dock in the world. Statements about vessels of exceptional (as distinct from merely large) size occur in the *Report of the Special Committee on Dock Extension* (1872), which was in effect a consultative draft of the Bill which became the 1873 Act, both of which retain such expressions as 'the free entry and working of the largest class of vessels'.

57 Hereafter, in the interests of brevity, dates are given as the year of publication of the Board's *Annual Acounts*.

58 Figures from G. J. Milne & G. Tonks, 'Specialised Port Facilities on Trial:Liverpool's Albert Dock in the Nineteenth Century' in A. Jarvis & K. Smith (Eds), *Albert Dock:Trade and Technology*, Liverpool, 1999

59 This does not, of course, mean that the Board was insolvent: it had other forms of income (notably from rents) which are excluded here because, varying little with trade activity, they do not serve as indicators of the success or otherwise of the business of the port.

60 Statements about the national state of trade here are from W. Page (ed), *Commerce and Industry* (1919) repr. New York, 1968. See Tables 56 (coal exports), 63 (Shipping), 5 (Emigration), 42 (Foodstuffs)

61 This question is considered in more detail in A. Jarvis, 'Port History: Some thoughts on where it came from and where it might be going' in L. R. Fischer & A. Jarvis (eds), *Harbours and Havens: Essays in Port History in Honour of Gordon Jackson*, St. John's Newfoundland, 1999.

62 First argued in detail in A. Jarvis, 'G. F. Lyster and the role of the Dock Engineer, 1861-97', *The Mariner's Mirror*, 78 (1992) 177-99.

63 Though without this restriction even Lyster's large team of engineers would have been severely stretched, and the ability to maintain trade by switching ships from one dock to another to avoid the works would also have been severely compromised.

64 Milne & Tonks, *op cit*

65 The yardstick figure in the *Engineer's Commonplace Book*, used for the roughest of 'ball-park estimates,' at this time was £20,000 per acre.

66 eg in 1885, £2.02 per square yard for single-storey, £4.95 per square yard for double. G. F. Lyster's *Commonplace Book*, (Eng 3/1), p62,

67 Ritchie-Noakes, *op cit*, pp68-70

68 Lyster's personal *Commonplace Book*, pp88-89.

69 G. F. Lyster, 'Recent Dock Extensions at Liverpool', *Min. Proc. ICE*, C (1889-90) pp2-114.

70 Or so he said in Lyster, 'Recent Dock Extensions': elsewhere he claimed they were bought for dumping dredgings.

71 Lyster's *Commonplace Book* pp88-89

72 Though the Board had a lengthy discussion on the subject at their meeting of 17 July 1890, reported in the verbatim sequence *Discussions at Board*.

73 One source of waste which Mr Glynn was keen to eliminate was the elaborate consultative process which preceded the 1873 Act, mentioned above. As he pointed out, the information then given to them was largely

worthless and was a large part of the reason for the now-acknowledged failure of the New North Works. (*Discussions at Board* 10 July 1890) The 1891 Bill went forward on the basis only of informal soundings of major customers, but it was, *mirabile dictu*, unopposed in Parliament.

74 For example, underpinning the walls of Huskisson and its No. 3 Branch cost £58 12s 6d per linear *foot*, making a total for the 21 acres of water of £243,201. Building a new wall of the considerable cross section of 70 square yards typically cost a little over £40 per linear foot at the time.

75 This was correctly anticipated by the Board on the basis of the success story at Coburg recounted below. (*Discussions at Board,* 17 July 1890) While Bramley-Moore did not profit greatly, Wellington's typical annual revenue rose from £12,000-£13,000 to around £18,000.

76 High water of neap tides.

77 For more on impounding pumps see 'Steam begat Steam', above.

78 These transactions are considered in greater detail in my paper 'Land Policies in the port of Liverpool 1857-1930', *International Journal of Maritime History*, XIV (2002), pp115-133.

79 Which was, in round figures, four times the cost per square yard of the shed to be built on some of it.

80 From 1836 until 1887 the published *Report of the Engineer* included a shortened version of his departmental accounts. After 1887 it is necessary to use the sequence mentioned, which consists of volumes binding together the new-style, purely narrative, *Report* with an MS copy of the accounts.

81 Another possibly telling comparison is that Liverpool's largest firm in the engineering sector (Mersey Steel and Iron Co. Ltd) had a total capital of £800,000.

82 See 'Steam begat Steam', above.

83 The floating plant was a special case: in the main, the Board did not insure it, carrying its own risks by putting aside a notional 'premium' and the depreciation allowance into what they confusingly called their 'insurance account'.

84 *op cit*

85 On the depreciation of dock works in general terms, see A. Jarvis, *The Liverpool Dock Engineers*, Stroud, 1996, Chapter 3.

86 Which is why Gladstone Dock, (designed 1910, completed 1927) with its huge entrance lock and sills 25ft below Old Dock Sill, eventually paid off by having a useful working life extending to the present day - and probably well beyond.

87 An earlier version of this paper was presented at the 'Maritime History beyond 2000' conference, Fremantle, 2001.

88 Cargo density was usually measured as the tonnage of cargo per foot length of the vessel.

89 Exceptionally, it was possible to carry out a modest scheme without going to Parliament, but for that the scheme had to be unopposed and funded from existing resources, with no new borrowing powers needed. The Queens Dock improvements recounted in the preceding paper are an example.

90 The attacks made on James Cropper are considered in A. Jarvis, 'James Cropper, Liverpool Docks and the Liverpool and Manchester Railway', *Journal of Transport History*, Third Series Vol. 19, 1998, pp18-32.

91 A. Jarvis, *The Liverpool Dock Engineers*, Stroud, 1996, pp 96-97.

92 eg W. G. Neale, *At the Port of Bristol*, (2 vols), Bristol, 1968; G. J. D. Tull, *The Port of London Authority*, London, 1959; S. Mountfield, *Western Gateway*, Liverpool, 1965.

93 The Canada - Huskisson improvements (1891-1901) cost £20,000 per water acre, and at their peak immobilised over 57 water acres. However, part of the reason for the high cost was the need to minimise occupation of berths.

94 See G. Milne & G. Tonks, 'Specialised Facilities on Trial: Liverpool's Albert Dock in the Nineteenth Century' in A. Jarvis & K. Smith (eds), *Albert Dock: Trade and Technology*, Liverpool, 1999.

95 An account of this work appears in Fielden Sutcliffe, 'Sundry Notes on Dock Construction', *Transactions of the Liverpool Engineering Society*, XXVI (1905), pp139-80.

96 *ibid*, contribution of Mr Kenyon to the discussion.

97 The depth of water available is more important for the length of time either side of high water during which the entrance can be used by average sized ships than for the ability to handle the occasional exceptionally large vessel.

98 The gates weighed 129 tons each. For the figures, see *Engineer's Commonplace Book No 1*, p49. There is some further detail in 'Steam

99 *Engineer's Reports* for those years. The tabulated data in the *Yearbook* refer to this project as 'Certain slight alterations at Canada Lock'!

100 The tonnages of the smaller ones are hard to find, but the total for dredgers alone was over 30,000 tons.

101 For further detail, see A. Jarvis, 'The "Fleet" of the Mersey Docks & Harbour Board', *Northern Seas Yearbook,* forthcoming. In practice they were often able to tie up two abreast.

102 Utilisation of the grab dredgers is difficult, perhaps impossible, to quantify. Costs of dredging of individual docks were reported, but statements as to what dredger did how much work in what length of time seem not to exist: they are provided only for the SPDs. What is clear is that the grab dredgers had very high maintenance requirements, suggesting that finding more than four of them actually at work at one time is unlikely.

103 These examples are from the *Engineer's Report* for the year in question.

104 Putting Princes Dock and East and West Waterloo out of commission, some 19 acres.

105 Such as casting large concrete blocks for building 'stanks' to form a temporary closure of an entrance.

106 eg in Jarvis, *Dock Engineers,* pages 122, 131,132, 143, 148.

107 Worked up paper 100/1 contains tender forms for the supply of coal which give estimated annual consumption at the various major delivery points for each year.

108 Estimated from minutes authorising the temporary closure of bridges, collected in WUP 146.

109 The examples below are drawn from WUP 141/1 and WUP162/1

110 Board, 16 May 1881.

111 These and many similar examples are to be found in WUP 120/1, *Wrecks in the docks.*

112 The 1874 Dock Act gave the Water Bailliff powers to raise or destroy any wreck which was a hazard to navigation and sell it and its cargo to meet the salvage costs, but the Board seems generally to have taken a lenient view if the wreck lay at a berth rather than in a passage or the body of a dock, often allowing owners time to arrange a cheaper salvage job for themselves. It is also open to question whether the vessels would in fact have realised enough to pay for the Water Bailliff's work.

113 Quay sweeping prior to 1912 worked under a complex system. The Board paid a contractor a set amount (typically about £1,200 pa) to sweep the quays and the contractor rebated part of that in consideration of the estimated value of such manure as he was able to separate out. In 1912, enraged by a sequence of strikes by carters, the Board took the work in-house and purchased three Yorkshire steam lorries for the purpose. One immediate result was the need for somewhere to keep and service the lorries. The story of quay-sweeping may be followed in WUP 207/1.

114 It should perhaps be explained that although Stanley Dock was pretty obsolete by then, the warehouses were still very much a going concern, yielding a profit that year of £14,754.

115 Bale bands were a particularly tiresome form of scrap, light in weight and springy.

116 The sale of old materials is documented in Worked-up Papers 58/1 and 58/2 (1876-1928) and continued in Unbound Worked-up Paper O14 vol III. Detailed citations are not given as the entries are in chronological order.

117 Much of the land on which London Docks were built, for example, was of low value until the docks were built. Liverpool had no choice but to build elaborate constructions on 'land and strand' sites because dry land sites were prohibitively expensive. (Though there were other reasons as well.)

118 The proceedings of the Special Committee, and minutes of deliberations on their proceedings, are in UWUP C169. It should be explained that although the Clarence system was tiny and obsolete, it was still intensively used by the coastwise trade and turned the surprisingly high total of 122 tons/quay yard/year - before one allows for some 40 yards used for rubbish.

119 Numerous examples in WUP 102/1, *Special Rent*, which is another testimony to clutter, offering such gems as the Chief Traffic Manager being authorised to destroy 'certain cases of tomatoes' which had simply been left by their owners to rot on the quay at Huskisson. (Traffic Committee 3 September, 1894)

120 WUP 100/1.

121 The Board's tendering procedure changed, making exactly comparable figures unobtainable, but during the coal strike of 1912 the Board of Trade enquired as to the Board's

coal stocks and was told that approximately 11,000 tons were on hand—though this admittedly followed some deliberate stocking-up in anticipation of the strike. (and, atypically, we are told where most of it was.) It was, however, said to be enough only for 4-5 weeks at the normal rate of consumption. WUP 100/1

122 There are many other unconsidered trifles which could be added here: for example, when the Waterloo Corn Warehouses were built it was assumed that much of the grain would be forwarded inland or coastwise still in bulk. In fact, for a long time most of what was discharged got bagged. No-one had thought to provide space for thousands of empty bags, which therefore added to the cluttering of working space.

123 A copy exists in WUP 203/1,

124 It is impossible to be precise because only occasionally do we know the exact area he was occupying, but see Appendix for one example.

125 I have not included allowances for vessels laid up, waiting for cargo or waiting to enter a graving dock, because these appear to be what one might term 'necessary waste' in the sense that the Board could not govern their incidence in any way.

126 As a simple example, the efficiency of Clarence, mentioned above as 122 tons/yd was really 125 tons/yard if we deduct the length of the rubbish depot's berth.

127 Based on the approximate cost of Toxteth Dock, 1888, at £50,000/acre.

128 In reality, as one would expect, the sailing tank ships hung on for years, indeed between 1900 and 1903 Anglo-American Oil Co. built six new four-masted barques of over 3,000 tons: B. Lubbock, *The Coolie Ships and Oil Sailers*, Glasgow, 1955, p118.

129 Little remembered today, Sir Boverton Redwood Bt. (1846-1919) was a prominent consulting chemist and engineer who held several offices in professional institutions and was advisor on petroleum matters to the Admiralty, Home Office, India office and Colonial Office. His entry in *Who was Who 1916-28* is among the longest in the volume.

130 For example, total imports rose from 73.9 million gallons in 1885 to 300.1 in 1905 and 488.1 in 1913. G. Jones, *The State and the Emergence of the British Oil Industry*, London, 1981, p32.

131 The diesel engine ignites its fuel purely by the heat developed on the compression stroke: the 'semi-diesel' runs in that way once started, but requires such expedients as external application of heat to make it start. Diesel's patent was granted in 1892, when semi-diesels had been made for some 20 years and the Akroyd Stuart design was in quite large-scale production.

132 P. B. Watson, 'Bulk Cargo Carriers' in R. Gardiner (ed), *The Golden Age of Shipping*, London, 1994.

133 Watson, *op cit*.

134 The main exceptions were at Avonmouth, Barry and Cardiff, all of which have a huge tidal range and Queen Elisabeth II dock at Eastham (Port of Manchester) where there is no deep water at all to be had at low tide.

135 For a detailed account of naval developments see G. Jones, *The State and the Emergence of the British Oil Industry*.

136 From some typescript sheets of information of forthcoming developments in the port, put together for a newspaper article. Works Committee Support Papers, 24 December 1919.

137 First report of the Departmental Committee on Petroleum Spirit, BPP 1910 cd 5175 XLIV. 609, at p20: 'Several witnesses had drawn attention to the dangers of this practice'. Nor was it just a passing fancy: one of those witnesses was the Coroner for Westminster, who referred to seven deaths spread over twelve years.

138 In 1900 just 175 motor vehicles were built in Britain: in 1907, 12,000; 1913, 34,000; 1924,147,000. S. P Ville, *Transport and the Development of the European Economy 1750-1918*, London, 1990, p180.

139 This does not mean that no petroleum distillation went on: it certainly did but the raw material was already a distillate, not crude.

140 This may be one reason why Liverpool's first purpose-built tanker berths (of which more below) were, atypically, upstream of the rest of the port: some pretty important people lived in the area beyond the downstream extremity of the port where one might otherwise have expected to find the tanker facilities.

141 Because, of course, barrels were prone to leaking.

142 For some further details of this site, see A. Jarvis, 'Land Policies in the Port of Liverpol, 1857-1930', *International Journal of Maritime History*, XIV (2002), pp115-133, and below.

143 These and similar figures below come from the MD&HB *Revenue Statements*

144 Though the *Dock Registers* reveal large registered tonnages of vessels light or in ballast, which were, of course, the customers for the four double-length graving docks.

145 Herculaneum had 596 yards of quay, Herculaneum Branch had 575.

146 Later, as oil-fired heating systems for offices and factories began to be adopted in the 1920s the autumn 'spike' grew.

147 One of these vehicles survives in the collections of National Museums & Galleries on Merseyside, Accession No. 1987-267.

148 The railway connection between the new jetty and the installations at Dingle Bank was completed in 1924: *Engineer's Report* for that year.

149 S. Mountfield, *Western Gateway*, Liverpool, 1964, pp 47, 51.

150 Foreign animals had by law to be landed at the designated Foreign Animals Wharf at Woodside, but the important Irish cattle trade was at this date 'coastwise' because Ireland was still part of the UK. Smaller numbers of Welsh and Scottish cattle were also imported.

151 See A. Jarvis, 'The Port of Liverpool and the Railway Companies', in P. Rees (ed) *Docks, Railways and the Movement of Goods: Papers presented at a Research Day School at Merseyside Maritime Museum*, Liverpool, 1994.

152 Shown in a site plan of the Shell-Mex depot, dated 1920. Parkhill House is still there. MD&HB drawings, Cabinet C3, Drawer 1.

153 In addition, some of the land mentioned below, bought from Mr Roberts in 1890 was let out for use as allotments and some of Old Woman's Hey as a sports field.

154 The Croppers were a successful Quaker merchant family of whom James, 1773-1840, was the best known. See K. Charlton, 'James Cropper (1773-1840) and Agricultural Improvement in the Early Nineteenth Century', *Transactions of the Historic Society of Lancashire and Cheshire*, 111 (1960) pp 65-78; K. Charlton, 'James Cropper and Liverpool's Contribution to the Anti-Slavery Movement', *ibid* 122 (1971), pp 57-80.

155 This was a murky and complex business: for futher details see A. Jarvis, 'Land Policies in the Port of Liverpool, 1857-1930, *International Journal of Maritime History*, forthcoming.

156 In fact the results were disappointing and the costs of dredging the Pluckington Bank to keep the Brunswick New Entrances (completed 1908) operable remained extremely heavy - in 1921, for example, they were significantly larger than the total revenue of Brunswick Dock.

157 UWUP T113.

158 *Engineering*, 22 July 1921 p158

159 The vague term 'anxious' is deliberately chosen: overall, the Board's trade grew strongly between 1900 and 1913, but there were many hiccups along the way - including the need to cease work on Gladstone 1908-10.

160 Unfortunately the Bill was unopposed, so there was no Select Committe enquiry into it. The evidence would have been extremely valuable.

161 *Engineer's Report and Accounts*, 1922, 1923, 1924. The shed in question was on the South Quay of Number 1 Branch.

162 No single storey sheds were built at a directly comparable time, but so long ago as 1903 the shed on the South Quay of Canada No 2 Branch cost £231 per linear yard. UWUP T683 Vol 2.

163 The first had been bought in 1925, following a hair-raising incident when sparks from a steam locomotive hauling tank wagons to Wapping Station set fire to the grass on the bank above Casemates 7 and 8! The Board's steam locomotives were, of course, fitted with spark arrestors but these were disliked by drivers as slowing steam generation When a hole burned in the middle of the spark arrestor, as it inevitably would at some stage, drivers often 'failed to notice'. This practice was widely known and allowing a locomotive in such a condition to work in a petroleum depot was imprudent.

164 There are two main sources for the generalisations in this paragraph: the *Weekly Returns* for the Jetty and the weekly summary of trade published in *Petroleum Times*. Unfortunately the former aggregates landings at the jetty, while the latter covers the Port as a whole (ie including the oil berths at the Great Float, Birkenhead. Confusion is compounded by the fact the *Weekly Returns* are given in tons and *Petroleum Times* worked in gallons: without knowing the specific gravity of each consignment one cannot convert from one to the other, though a figure of 0.8 was sometimes used as a rough average.

165 *Petroleum Times*, 20 May 1922, p701.

166 'Large' at this time meant about 500ft long. The drawing is in the 'Dingle Oil Installations' portfolio, Cabinet C3, drawer 31.

167 Weekly Return of vessels using the jetty: Docks & Quays Committee Support Papers, September 1926.

168 A. C. Hardy, *Bulk Cargoes*, London, 1926.

169 Pumpfields Power Station, 1901 (8.4 MW) and Lister Drive No3, 1926 (58 MW) may stand as examples of respectively the second and third generations of station.

170 D. F. Dixon, 'Petrol Distribution in the United Kingdom, 1900-1950', *Business History*, VI No 1 (December 1963) pp1-19.

171 There is one small exception: the sequence of *Dock Revenue Statements* has separate figures for Dingle jetty for 1924 only, but even that does not help us with the tonnages or revenues at other berths, notably Herculaneum Branch.

172 The distinction between Dock Dues and Town Dues had been meaningless since 1857, but for reasons I have never seen explained they continued to be calculated separately. The rates given here are those for 1923.

173 Using the jetty probably cost more in tug hire, but that was a matter between the shipowner and the tug-owner in which the Board was not involved.

174 The only source which reveals time spent at discharging berths is the notoriously unwieldy *Dock Registers*. (*Lloyds List* and the *Bills of Entry* do not normally record movements within the port) This statement is not based on systematic analysis but only on a series of spot checks made at a number of dates and at different times of year. The difference is obvious. It should remembered that although tankers at this time only discharged at around 300 tons/hour, once they were connected to the hoses they discharged without stopping for lunch, bad weather or the night.

175 This is an interesting sidelight: the port's trade did not plummet, it merely fluctuated a little and on balance stagnated. Liverpool's borrowing policy however had been predicated since at least the 1840s on more or less continuous growth: against such aspirations stagnation represented a near-disaster.

176 The sale of Clarence Dock to the Corporation to build a power station helped, but the Board's debt still rose from £35.3 million in 1929 to £37.1 million in 1932.

177 The 'Anyport model' represents a typical pattern of port development over time: it appears in J. Bird, *The Major Seaports of the United Kingdom*, London, 1963.

178 G. C. Allen *et al*, *The Import Trade of the Port of Liverpool: Future Prospects*, Liverpool, 1946.

179 Including the construction of Princes Dock between the commencement of works in late 1811 and the end of the wars in 1815.

180 This was to keep the works at Gladstone (which, contrary to popular belief, never *entirely* stopped) moving on. The costs of accommodating, feeding and guarding the prisoners were problematical, and the Board last discussed the issue on 8 November 1918.

181 A point of view on which he later expanded in G. Jackson, 'Ports, Ships and Government in the nineteenth and twentieth centuries', in P. C. van Royen *et al*, (eds), *Frutta di Mare: Evolution and Revolution in the Maritime World in the 19th and 20th Centuries*, Amsterdam, 1998.

182 Any c.1900 edition of The *Shipping World Year Book* will give a flavour of this diversity. For a comparative appraisal of the major forms of ownership see A. Jarvis, 'Managing Change: The Organisation of Port Authorities at the Turn of the Twentieth Century', *The Norther Mariner/Le Marin du nord*, VI, (1996), 31-42.

183 In fairness it must be conceded that the enquiries of the *Royal Commission on Labour* did investigate dock labour.

184 *Royal Commission to Enquire into the Administration of the Port of London*, BPP 1902 (1151) XLIII.222

185 BPP 1903, LXIII.189

186 Perhaps the most important of those not cited below were the two Select Committee Enquiries into the Causes of Shipwrecks, BPP 1836 (567) XVII. 373 and BPP 1843 (581) IX. 669.

187 This theme may be traced from Tudor times onwards in D. J. Starkey (ed), *England's Sea Fisheries*, London, 2000.

188 'Fishermen are the peasant farmers of the sea. They are scattered along the margin of their domain... To supersede these by large firms concentrated at a few ports would alter the character of the fishermen and thereby injure a very important element of our national strength.' *Report of the Treasury Committee to consider questions relating to the Employment of Convicts in the UK*, BPP 1882 (c3427) XXXIV.649, appendix 4.

189 BPP 1859 (2474) X Pt.1.1, which also followed

on the findings of the *Royal Commission on Tidal Harbours*, whose second report is in BPP 1846 XVIII Pt1. 1.

190 See *Select Committee on Local Charges on Shipping*, BPP 1856 (332) XII.1.

191 *Treasury Committee to Consider Questions Relating to the Employment of Convicts in the United Kingdom*, BPP 1882 (c3427) XXXIV.649: Evidence of Sir John Coode.

192 A. G. L Shaw, *Convicts and the Colonies*, London, 1966, gives a long view from the first shipments to North America to the end of transportation.

193 'The great bulk of the technical innovations were directed more at ways to better calculate treadwheel labor and dissipate the power...' D. H. Shayt, 'Stairway to Redemption: America's Encounter with the British Prison Treadmill', *Technology & Culture*, 30 (1989), 908-38.

194 *Treasury Committee Report...* p656.

195 'Bagwork' involved filling huge bags (up to 50 tons) with concrete which was allowed to set partially then laid in the water by a crane or traveller, where it deformed while setting to make a sound bond with those below and around it. There is an enormous professional literature on the development of concrete technique at this period: the interested reader should refer to the Subject Index for Volumes I-LVIII of *Min Proc ICE*.

196 *Report of Sub Committee to investigate the most suitable place for a Harbour of Refuge on the East Coast of Scotland, to be constructed by Convicts* BPP 1884 (c4035) XLIII.289, at p14.

197 A view which emerges clearly in the Report of the *Select Committee on Railway Labour*, BPP 1846 (530) XIII.425

198 *Royal Commission to Enquire into the Operation of Acts relating to Transportation and Penal Servitude*, BPP 1863 (3190) (3190-I) XXII.283, q2298.

199 For further details of this argument, see K. Charlton, 'James Cropper and Liverpool's Contribution to the Anti-slavery Movement', *Transactions of the Historic Society of Lancashire and Cheshire*, 122 (1971), 57-80.

200 Assessing and optimising the performance of manual labour was a matter of considerable interest to engineers, see, for example, J. Farey, 'On Mr Smeaton's "Estimates of Animal Power" extracted from his MS papers', *Min Proc ICE* II (1839), 50, which also refers to figures worked out by Desaguliers. W. J. M.

Rankine's classic textbook *The Steam Engine and other Prime Movers* (numerous editions from 1859 onwards) has a section on the subject.

201 Convict labour was used in the Royal Dockyards as well.

202 *Select Committee to inquire into the policy of making further Grants of Public Money for Improvement and Extension of Harbours of Refuge* BPP 1857 Session 2 (262) XIV.1, qq1527-28.

203 *ibid*, q1699.

204 The only copy of this report I have seen is in the Institution of Civil Engineers Archives, Tracts Folio, Vol 7, item 4.

205 The reader will by now have realised that Sir John Coode (1816-92, knighted 1872) became something of a specialist in the use of convict labour. He was a pupil of James Meadows Rendel and worked as a consultant during the railway mania. In 1847 he went to work as resident under Rendel at Portland Harbour, and for the rest of his life was engaged mainly in harbour works in many different countries around the world. His output may be judged from the unusal length of his obituary in *Min Proc ICE* CXIII (1893), pp334-42.

206 See, for example, the evidence of 'A.B.', an ex-convict, before the Royal Commission on Penal Servitude.

207 One major reason for this was to prevent free workers selling tobacco to convicts: it was estimated that allowing convicts to have tobacco could have increased output by up to 30% (*Enquiry into ... Transportation and Penal Servitude*, q5943), but output was not the point.

208 A. R. Buchan, 'Peterhead, Scotland's 100-year Harbour of Refuge', *Proc ICE Pt 1*, 1984, 76, 681-96, provides a detailed account together with references to the considerable quantity of Parliamentary Papers generated over the century.

209 *Report of Treasury Committee* p687. Out of sixteen suggestions for 'disciplinary occupation', eleven were for harbour works.

210 Though it has to be admitted that Dupin's larger work, *Voyages dans La Grande Bretagne* (1824) has been cited in, for example, A. W. Skempton, 'Engineering in the Port of London, 1789-1808', *Transactions of the Newcomen Society*, 50 (1978-79), pp87-108, without becoming widely known.

211 See J. R. Harris, *Industrial Espionage and Technology Transfer*, Aldershot, 1998.

212 This was, of course, something of an

exaggeration, possibly prompted by the fact that harbour improvements begun at Whitehaven in 1815 had run out of money in 1817-18.

213 On *Etna* and her contemporaries, see A. J. Scarth, 'Early Mersey Steamships' in H. M. Hignett (ed), *A Second Merseyside Maritime History*, Liverpool, 1991.

214 J. R. Harris, *op cit.*

215 Counter-cyclical spending (not, of course, known by that name) occurred at various other stages in the history of the port, most spectacularly during the great financial crisis of 1847-48. For details: A. Jarvis, 'Port History: Some Thoughts on Where it Came from and Where it Might be Going', in L. R. Fischer & A. Jarvis (eds) *Harbours and Havens: Essays in Port History in Honour of Gordon Jackson*, St. John's, 1999.

216 And even then it was not complete: the last finishing touches were not applied until 1825.

217 For details, see A. Jarvis, *Liverpool Central Docks 1799-1905*, Stroud, 1991, Chapter 2, Section 2.

218 John Foster had six sons, of whom William acted as his assistant and later became Secretary to the Dock Committee, Thomas became Town Clerk, and John Junior Borough Surveyor.

219 Some stone from Runcorn was also used, and in the early stages of construction stone also came from the old Corporation Quarries.

220 Though it should be added that technical drawing skills were not widespread in England at the time. See P. J. Booker, *A History of Engineering Drawing*, London, 1979.

221 N. Ritchie-Noakes, *Liverpool's Historic Waterfront*, London, 1984, 163

222 This is only speculation: there is no proof that Aydon & Elwell cast the bridge at Wapping. However, the nose castings of the leaves had to be subtly formed to prevent the bridge jamming, making possession of the patterns a considerable asset.

223 Though at a later date his nephew, James Walker, did.

224 On the issue of Rennie and Walker generally, see Skempton, *op cit*

225 A. W. Skempton, (ed), *Biographical Dictionary of Civil Engineers*, Vol 1, London, 2000, entry for Ralph Walker.

226 *ibid*, Appendix 1.

227 This, of course, is not correct: the crucial distinction is that Liverpool's was the first *commercial* wet dock.

228 The inclusion of Lancaster, which was not an important manufacturing centre, is puzzling.

229 The Douglas Canal had in fact been incorporated (both organisationally and physically) into the Leeds & Liverpool by this date.

230 These are Metric leagues of 4 kilometres or 2.5 miles, making the distance 3.75 miles.

231 These are not included here, being readily obtainable elsewhere.

232 And, of course, it suffered quite severe structural and financial problems.

233 Not for nothing was the flight officially called 'Cheshire Locks' known to boatmen as 'Heartbreak Hill': it was not really a flight at all, its locks strung out half a mile here, a mile there.